Permis

In 60 Thoughts
Bernadette Petrie

Shine and from here all good will come! things

with love
Bernadette

Seaweed Press

Published in 2019 by Seaweed Press

ISBN Paperback: 978-1-9161168-0-1
Ebook: 978-1-9161168-1-8

A CIP catalogue copy of this book can be found in the British Library.

Edited by Kim Williams
Cover design by So It Begins
Cover photograph by Amanda Farnese Heath

Published with the help of Indie Authors World

IndieAuthors
World

Dedication

Mammas and Papas said it best, so like them this book "is dedicated to the ones I love"– those little ones who cracked me open, Jessica and Flynn, and their now bigger selves, who keep it real and inspire me to be the best version of me I can be.

Contents

Foreword

This book's purpose is to encourage you to give yourself permission to be fully yourself by loving and accepting all parts of you. I feel we all have access to the Source of life, which resides inside us – and our life force is everything. But we have to accept who we fully are, to experience it.

Throughout this book I refer to God, Source, the Universe, Divinity, Consciousness, Grace and sometimes Nature. Frequently I will use the words Love and Energy. So it's worth spending a moment to explain, as best I can, what I mean by these terms.

Essentially to me they all mean the same thing.

I grew up in a religious environment and always believed in something bigger. But that 'God' or what I was conditioned to believe God was, appeared to me in 2010 very differently. I had the 'God thing' all wrong it seems. I am very aware that when I say the word 'God' because of different experiences or thoughts, we are not necessarily thinking about the same thing, because now God means something very different to me.

I don't desire any religious labels, or any labels for that matter. Religion is a concept created by humans, not by God. At the origin of all religions the truth probably does reside, but in this book I am referring to the overriding Source of all of us.

I use the words God and Source in the context of what I have come to experience as energy, a Glorious Onward Direction. The Source of all life, which means Nature, Love, Divinity, Energy, The Universe and Consciousness are used with the same intention. Can any one word truly contain this essence?

Following my experience in 2010 I discovered new words that felt to me to be better descriptions of what I had formerly thought of as God, words like Source, Divinity, Energy, Grace, Love and

Consciousness. The God word and our misunderstanding of it, is however the source of our suffering. I use it to get you questioning everything, because to me, it is literally 'everything'.

I also refer to God sometimes as a 'she' because I experienced guidance in a female voice and I'm female. As Neale Donald Walsh says in 'Conversations with God'; "God speaks to us in our own voice".

I would love this book to help you to become more curious about what your life force is and if any of these words are a trigger I encourage you to dive a bit deeper and question your own thoughts about this.

Every life force has a Source, let me help you give yourself permission to let yours guide you onwards.

A MIRACLE OF GRAVITY

As you weave the letters of your life,
don't forget the toil and strife.

Don't forget the loss and pain,
and let's remember all the shame.

But please remember, to look behind,
and see the light that shines and shines.

As you weave your web of life,
a miracle of gravity,
The light, that glimmers glistens and glows,
in the dark in the midst of chaos knows,
of a story brave and bold and free,
so weave this life for you and me.

Weave and weave it BIG and BOLD,
this life of yours must be told.

Introduction

This life of mine began in 1969 in Northern Ireland. A time in Northern Irish history that would become known as 'The Troubles'. Where an almost invisible to the outside eye religious divide, as seen in many other parts of the world too, would try to destroy the very essence of the love that runs deep within all the people there. Born into a Catholic family in a largely Protestant housing development, in a largely Protestant town and county, I would become the middle child of a large much loved family and I was from the age of 10 very much in all things Bernadette in the middle.

In the middle of my family, in the middle of religious understanding, in the middle of both, Catholic and Protestant friends, and later, I always felt very much in the middle of two very different perspectives everywhere I went.

Now I can see that all this was meant to be – I chose it all and I did so for a bigger purpose. I chose this experience to play my part in shining a light on the millions of unquestioned thoughts that drive our behaviour and the thousands of limiting beliefs that cause us to let 'fear' not 'faith' guide us onwards. My personal experience of depression, which I now consider the 'human condition', helped me to finally wake up because without 'an emotional education' we really have been ill-prepared to step into the darkness of our own psyche and discover our light Source.

We need to look at all of these things so we can free ourselves from thinking: "*We are not enough, we are not wholly loveable, we are not powerful.*"

Most importantly we have to extinguish the lie that runs throughout humanity. The lie that would stop me from sharing all of these things with you. The lie that we are afraid of our dark, when the truth is we are actually afraid of our light. Once we get a glimpse and start to believe something better about ourselves, the journey of loving and cherishing ourselves fully can truly begin.

On 20th July 2010 at the age of 41 I was admitted to the Glasgow Priory. It was day five of a roller-coaster journey that had frightened people close to me and their fear had terrified the heck out of me. I was mentally and physically exhausted. Why? Because this intensive five-day awakening process meant my whole life finally made sense, every single detail and I felt wholly accountable.

I needed desperately to sleep and I was so relieved to be going somewhere, where I envisioned peaceful angels taking care of me. Beings, that were, not afraid to look into my eyes, who would simply lovingly hush my chatter by giving a knowing smile to reassure me. I needed to let go of being 'in control' and felt sure this, was where this would finally happen.

My late evening arrival proved inconvenient for the staff, as it was shift change-over time. A doctor I would never see again hurriedly performed blood pressure and heart rate checks. She asked my husband to leave the room for a few moments and as he did I felt myself starting to let go. This proved short-lived as he was understandably keen to be with me and decided to return. I remember pulling myself together, trying to remain strong so as not to upset him. He'd had a roller-coaster ride too and I felt sure he, too, could do with a host of angels. It was only when I was finally alone that the reality hit me. I was in a psychiatric hospital thought to be mentally unstable and a danger to myself. Yet even though I knew I was on the edge of something major and it scared me, I knew it wasn't the case. I had been a danger to myself. I had been my own worst enemy for far too long. Now I knew I couldn't turn back. The chain of events from the previous summer, were no coincidence. I was also sure that the fact I was back in Glasgow, only a few moments from where I had lived in my twenties, wasn't a coincidence either. We really do come full circle to rediscover ourselves.

I unpacked my clothes and a few personal items, which my husband had so thoughtfully packed. I had a shower, putting on new white PJs that a dear friend had sent me and I climbed into bed. I remember looking at my favourite picture of my husband and the kids, taken one mother's day and becoming upset. I got out of bed and turned it over, telling myself that in order to be able to love and take care of them fully, I needed to really take care of myself and trust that this was all happening for a reason.

I turned out the light and closed my eyes trying to sleep, uncertain of what the morning would bring. It was then, the chest pains that had been coming and going in the previous days returned, stronger than ever before. I was totally confused. Who was I worried about now? The kids were safe, so was my husband. I had surrendered my business commitments, I had no more secrets and yet the chest pain continued.

I said these words out loud. "God I'm done you'll have to take it from here" I wasn't sure what or who God was but because I had nothing left in me, I fully let go.

Suddenly the chest pains were replaced by an incredible feeling of warmth and my entire body became a ball of light. I felt the presence of two more balls of light in the room with me. To this day, I don't know where it began and ended. But what I felt sure was that, in this act of total surrender I was returning home. This experience was life changing for me. It's like there was Bernie before the Priory and Bernie after.

In that weightless experience I was beautifully reminded that Source is in and around us always. It's only our thinking that makes us feel it's not. I could have stayed in that ball of loving light forever because in that moment of surrender, I rejoiced in the returning home to the truth that God had been inside of me all along. There really is no place like home.

But Source had other plans. A voice from deep inside me, a female voice, strong and certain, spoke only for a few seconds; "Call out for help, call out for help now."

As I did, I found myself crashing to the floor unable to move. Two nurses who had by now rushed to my room tried to get me to stand up, but I was like a dead weight. The male nurse said; "Get up, get up, you've got to get up. You're going to frighten the other patients". Just about able to speak I said; "I can't get up and I don't care about the other patients".

By calling out for help and crashing to the floor I had been given a fresh chance to start living honestly all over again, but this time, with the memory of who we truly are, once again intact. In that moment it felt like that floor had been waiting for me my whole life.

The message I received was - It's here in our everyday lives where we have to continue the courageous work. We have to be willing to step into our light and continue to let it shine. We have to be courageous and let ourselves shine, and we can only do that by loving and cherishing, and bringing home all parts of ourselves. We need to allow Source to guide us every step of the way. Those 'parts of us' are parts that are stuck in the middle of our old story. We have to save them so they can return home to the present moment with us.

As I sat on the bed supported by the nurses my whole body started to shake and all I wanted was water. I discovered later, this is quite typical after a spiritual awakening, which is effectively an intense energetic healing. I drank glass after glass with the nurses' help. I remember one of them scolding me; *"You've got to think of your family, you can't be doing this to yourself"*. I was dumbfounded, but of course they had no idea of what had just happened, I had been totally alone. Even if I could have explained it I doubt they would have believed me. I'm not sure I would have if I had been in their shoes.

I remembered thinking; *"Oh no you don't understand, I'm so lucky I have remembered it's all going to be okay now"*. I felt so, so happy even if I had been zapped of all physical strength. I fell asleep only waking to ask for more water throughout the night. I would continue to sleep on and off almost solidly, for the next four days.

On my third or fourth day of my stay in the Priory, I remember glancing in the mirror as I walked to the bathroom stooped like an old lady. My body was clearly in need of physical recovery, because my mind had been cracked open yet my heart was full of love. I knew that truth and faith, not just fear, were my new companions.

It would be six weeks before I returned home. During this time I realised that certain parts of me, my inner child parts especially, were not up to speed with this new perspective. And so began the long slow journey of living with my eyes open to this truth, although certain parts were still in fear. For the last nine years I've let life lead me and when the need arose I've been diving deep to rediscover the parts of me still hiding in the dark, and in doing so I have helped others do the same.

SECTION ONE

Love and cherish

SOMETIMES

Sometimes I'm my own worst enemy
I'm the one who lets me down
I'm the one who steals my passion
And scolds me when I frown.

I'm the one who trips me up,
steals my joy and taints my love.
I'm the one who when my back
is turned is giving me a shove.

It suddenly feels cluttered,
my hearts no longer full
With spaces of my mind jam-packed
creativity is nil.

It's because my thoughts are cluttered
That it's not easy to find
the creativity that's inside me
It's as if – suddenly I'm blind.

Then comes pause...

I take a deep breath
And lean inside
And let my inner wisdom rear,
and like a spring cleaning Ninja
watch my mental cobwebs disappear.

Embrace and know all the parts of you
that you would rather hide away
Let them come out, but teach them how to play.

They just need some guidance from beginning to end
Which is why you must always be,
your own best friend.

Slow down sweetheart there is no need to rush

One day my son hopped into the car beside me and said; *"Mum, I can't wait until I'm taller than you"*. He was about half an inch away. When I started to write this book, nine months later, he had overtaken me by a good couple of inches. But as I sat in the car that morning, his words made me smile. Yet I also felt for him, remembering, all too well, the angst of teenage growing years. In his race to manhood, his height is ever present – the rush to leave childhood spurring him on. A few weeks before, he had asked if he could go to Amsterdam for the day with his friends (he was 14) and I heard myself saying to him; *"Slow down sweetheart there is no need to rush."*

I am very aware that the full expression of who he is to be, will involve significant changes, not just physical, over the next few years. And there are stages and steps he will need to take, which will enable him to expand his world and do all the things he seems desperate to do right now. Whilst the physical changes seem more obvious at his age and stage, the full expression of who I am to be in the future also involve me growing, stretching and continuing beyond my comfort zone too.

The message is the same; *"Slow down sweetheart there is no need to rush"*. Do it step-by-step, day-by-day.

Over a nine month period, I doodled 277 flower doodles, one every day almost like daily meditation. Then one day I didn't. I had shared them on Instagram as I doodled. I used them in workshops and I've given many of the original doodles to clients and started to refer to them as divinity cards. My desire was to explore the thoughts whispered to me by Source, illustrated in the form of flower doodles. The doodles throughout this book will take you on an internal journey, enabling you to bring some of those parts of yourself home and as you do, you will get their permission to shine.

In the following chapters, with the flower doodles to guide us, we will begin by unraveling when and why we become so afraid of the very light that we are. We will look at how it is possible for us to be our own best friend, and love and cherish all parts of who we are. Next, we will look at our dreams and what we secretly want, and finally discover that it is our birthright to shine as brightly as we can. All possible by stepping back from lies, into the true awareness of who we are.

Take your time with this book. Engage with it, do the exercises, trust when to pick it up and when to put it down. When we rush we miss all these beautiful uplifting moments, so *slow down sweetheart there is no need to rush*".

2

Love and cherish who you are right now

I was given a special gift several years ago when out walking on the beach with one of my dearest friends. We had met as first-time expectant mothers when my husband and I were living on the west coast of Scotland and had became friends as we birthed and bonded over many child rearing moments. I was obviously giving myself a hard time because what she said stayed with me and was one of those pivotal comments that sent me on an inner enquiry. "*Do you know what your problem is Bernie? You are your own worst enemy.*"

My question as we start this journey together is; "*are you your own worst enemy?*" Is there really anyone who is meaner to you, than you are to yourself? How do you talk to yourself? Refer to yourself? Push yourself? Treat yourself? Just how different would you feel, if you loved and cherished who you are, and accepted and loved everything about you, including your body, your voice your everything?

What if you loved and appreciated everything about you, as a human being, and if you loved and appreciated your actual body, and reconsidered it as a vehicle to be cared for, rather than as all that you are?

What if it's an avatar that you have been given for this earth experience, as you walk along your very own yellow brick road?

This avatar is a precious thing and it enables you to experience exactly what you are meant to be experiencing, meaning you have never left the source of who you truly are.

How you feel in the body, in the skin that you are in, is all feedback and the path will look brighter or duller depending on how tuned into your body you actually are. The feedback you are feeling and experiencing, is a result of all your thoughts and the beliefs you currently hold onto. What you do with that feedback is entirely up to you. You get to choose every step of your earth bound way.

Just as Dorothy from the 'Wizard of Oz' (yes, I'm a total movie buff) finally realised, this is your show and you have all the guidance you will ever need right inside you. You have the ability to shape and create your reality by questioning all of your beliefs and thoughts.

In the powerful life changing moment alone in my room in the Priory I was fully broken from the shackles of the thoughts and beliefs that had steered my entire life. And I can only conclude that I saw a glimpse of my truth, I saw, who I truly was.

In the weeks and months after my stay at the Priory, while I was recuperating from the physical experience of my awakening, I researched other people's experiences and the physical effects it had on them. Not everyone agreed with me about the whole 'awakening' idea and I experienced massive changes in my energy levels. This really confused me, and in the days, weeks and months that followed I was often filled with fear and uncertainty, which felt childlike at times.

It became clear that whilst I had been given a new perspective, something old was still very much playing in the background. I was yet to understand that there was much more for me to learn about taking responsibility for my own energy field and that I really need to demonstrate love and compassion to all parts of me.

My curiosity has always been a big part of my makeup and I had previously considered being nosey, a flaw. But during my time in the Priory I decided to dig deeper and use my God-given curiosity to figure out just what the heck was going on. Why did I suddenly feel like a frightened little girl when I heard angry male voices? Why did

I still feel I needed to please other people all the time? This curiosity served me well and I ask you to bring to mind a flaw of your own. Take a look at it from another perspective. This flaw I believe, will be one of your essential self-loving enablers.

My story is not one of instantaneously 100% enlightenment. Mine is a story of how to heal thoughts and beliefs, one step at a time. How we can actually follow our own yellow brick road. This was my mission, impossible at times, often sabotaged by my own thoughts and beliefs.

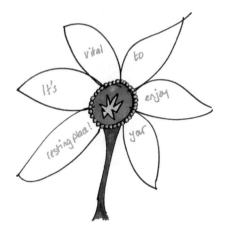

3

It's Vital to enjoy your resting place

It would take over a year, after leaving the Priory before I felt fully physically strong, and by then I realised that I was really just getting started.

Loving and cherishing who you are, is a life's work! It's part of the mission and it's the conduit to our healing and our joy.

I am a fairly regular climber of our local hill called The Law. A few years ago I found myself chuckling as I started my climb. A new sign had popped up at the start of the trail. It said 'Summit Path' with an arrow pointing in the correct direction, clearly there, to guide newbies in the right direction.

The reason I chuckled is that The Law, is less than 200 metres to the top and it takes 15 to 20 minutes to get to the summit. This is not to be underestimated, mind, I puff and pant every time I climb it, and by the end of this particular climb I would come to think of 'the summit' somewhat differently.

When I think of other much bigger hills and Munros I have scaled, I have to admit to being a very grumpy climber; "*Are we there yet? This is hard! Why, why?*" Back then, I did not think – I have chosen this life and these hills are my powerful teachers. I think about being that young woman often and so seeing this sign made me giggle all the more. Boy-oh-boy, I use to make things really hard for myself.

After I had been climbing for about ten minutes, I became lost in thought, it happens every time. When I looked up and I saw I was off track, it took me a few seconds to find a path again and see the summit once more. I had, before this point, rested for a few seconds here and there, but with new focus I made a final non-stop push to the top – to 'the summit'. Once there, I realised the message. When you get to the actual top of a climb, without question, that is the resting place. It is from there you get to see an expanded view of your world and there is no more climbing to do. You just have to be with it. You cannot physically climb any higher.

This is exactly like our spiritual journey. If we ignore the resting place, and are constantly climbing, climbing, climbing, we are never actually at peace with who we are, where we are, and that place of striving – we are missing the point.

Each time I climb The Law I let more baggage go. When I get to the top I see something new, and so each time I have a new level of understanding about my life. I'm a different version of me each time I climb, there is no need for the Law to get bigger – the expansion happens on the inside.

When I get to the top, there is no more climbing to be done that day, on that hill of doubt. I need to focus on the resting place and reconnect with my current life – see it through this new lens.

I encourage you to climb your hill of doubt, and only climb it when you want to. I encourage you to take breaks along the way, but when you get to the place that feels like a for-now resting place – rest!

Rest, savour the life you see below, appreciate all that it is showing you, and in that moment of acceptance and appreciation you will discover that you have expanded just perfectly.

You will be climbing this hill of doubt again and again, for ever more, but only because you want to. Remembering that, will make, all the difference.

As I write today, in 2019, I'm nowhere done but I realise that it's not about the destination, it's about the experiences along each and every one of our earth bound days that we need to embrace and treasure, and in the process resist the temptation to strive endlessly for a dizzy spiritual height that would detach us from our humanity. From who we are on this earth, right here, right now.

Being human, an awake human with your own Source energy, is really something to treasure. You are exactly where you are meant to be, nothing has gone wrong and you are definitely not, in the true sense, broken. We may be fragmented, parts of us are hiding in the dark and we are in denial of parts that we need to own. But we reclaim those parts day-by-day when we love and cherish who we are right now.

4

Hold your beliefs loosely in your hands

If I close my eyes I can still see her stillness as she led a mindfulness session at the Priory – her name was Sharon. I don't know her surname and weirdly when I looked back at my journal I've no mention of her. But I think of her words frequently and consider her one of my early spiritual guides when I awoke to a new reality in July 2010.

The fact she was Irish was a lovely bonus. Sharon seemed to have the incredible ability to thread beautiful lessons in fly away like comments. I remember saying to her one afternoon that I wouldn't make one of her classes but that I would be there in spirit. She smiled warmly and said; "I think you'll find it wise to take your spirit with you Bernie." Isn't it amazing how we throw around our words without fully understanding the energetic meaning, and isn't it incredible how a couple of comments can steer you back on course? She is probably unaware of the profound affect she had on me, and I will always think of her as one of my guardian angels – her Divinity shone brightly.

It was in her first class that I heard the words; "*hold your beliefs loosely in your hands*". I went on to share these words with my clients and have written about them in my blog. I work daily to embody them again and again. They are a constant reminder to me, on each and every step of this human journey.

As she sat quietly, legs crossed on the floor, in front of a small group of us she held a book loosely in her hands. As she did so, her hands were in an upward facing open position. Very gently she opened with this sentence; *"As you walk through this life I encourage you from here on in to hold your beliefs' loosely in your hands."*

Because when we hold onto to any beliefs tightly, there is no room for growth, change, or expansion. The energy is one of fear and the results are often limiting. When we hold onto a belief tightly we might be right but does it feel good in your body to hold onto something this tightly? It will start to get exhausting. Even the beliefs I have today, I realise, I must hold loosely in my hands because life is always revealing another perspective, and what was true for me today may no longer be true for me in the future. My expansion depends on that space – that freedom to explore.

One of the stories that illustrated this for me was the belief that the earth was flat. This now seems ludicrous, yet this belief was as strong and as real as many of the personal beliefs we may hold today. This belief was based on fear and hearsay and it kept people safe. Those that disregarded this strongly held belief were considered mad. But as more and more people questioned it, the tipping point came, and the rest is history. But those who held onto the belief rigidly never did experience the New World.

We constantly have the opportunity to step into a newer world. A more expanded human experience, as long as we remember to continue to hold any of the beliefs that guide us gently, so we can always question them and update them, allowing room for our natural expansion as we journey onwards in this magical Universe.

Whatever beliefs you are holding today in your hands – hold them loosely so that you can see them from all angles. And if fear pops up remember those brave adventurers who ventured off in large ships to the edge of the world, and take a step towards your own adventure.

What you believe matters.

Just what are your beliefs? Take a moment to write down, beliefs you hold about: you, life, love, money, sexuality, spirituality and relationships. If other headings pop up, as relevant to you, write down beliefs about those. It will be interesting to discover what you currently believe.

Since my time in the Priory many of the books I have read have mirrored my new realisations and reflections. In '*Change your Words, Change your World*' Andrea Gardner wrote; "*Beliefs, give rise to thoughts, and words, which birth, our actions*".

This is exactly what I had dramatically woken up to in 2010. It all starts with 'beliefs'. Andrea is now someone I consider a soul sister, and there is rarely a week that goes by when I'm not repeating the above line to myself.

If, for example, one of your limiting thoughts is; "*I am not good enough*". You will probably resist putting yourself forward for a promotion, a new job or any exciting opportunity or experience. These thoughts could stop you from reaching out and making contact with a potential new friend. You may also, because of a limiting belief, stop yourself speaking up or sharing on a forum. They could prevent you from taking action, when your actions or words could make all the difference to someone or a situation. The thought; "*I am not enough*", prevents other people benefiting from the gifts that only you can give them. It also prevents people who inspire you from coming into your life, thereby limiting the levels of joy in your life, whether it, be emotionally, financially or spiritually.

Believing limiting thoughts keeps you stuck, afraid, shrunk – that doesn't feel good does it? But, what if you questioned these self-limiting beliefs one-by-one? After all how can you be 100% sure that they are even true? The importance of questioning beliefs, reminds me of a sweet and simple story I heard many years ago. This story illustrates how important it really is, to question everything:

A young child was watching her mother prepare the Sunday roast. She watched her mother cut off part of the roast and set it to one side. Puzzled, she asked; "*Mummy, why do you do that?*" Her mother opened her mouth to reply, then stopped, and said; "*Do you know what honey, I have no idea why, it's just something my mother always did, so I do it too.*" Grandmother was there that day; so the mother and young child asked her, the same question; *"Grandma, you know when you are preparing the roast, why do you chop off part of it?"*

Grandma, goes to speak, and then stops and says; *"Do you know, I have absolutely no idea, it was what my mother always did, so I did it too, but actually now that you ask I have no idea why."*

Totally curious, they decide to ring up Great-Grandmother and ask her; *"Grandma we were wondering why did you cut off the end of the roast? It turns out we've been doing, without question, for years, but now that Amy has asked us why, we can't answer her and we realised we never asked you why"*. Great-Grandma is silent for a moment or two then, comes the roar of laughter. Finally, giggling, she says; *"My roasting dish was too small, so I had to."*

Question your beliefs that create your actions. Do this continually as what was true for then, is not necessarily true now or going to serve you or others one little bit. Is it time to look at your list of beliefs, and question them? The beliefs you are currently living your life with, could be nothing to do with you at all, and therefore need reassessing.

This never stops. Remember when people believed the world was flat, and because this was eventually questioned, the world as we saw it, changed.

Celebrate your uniqueness every single day

Have you ever considered if what you see in the mirror is different to what other people see? What if they see and experience a really beautiful essence shining through your avatar, and it is your limiting beliefs about your self that prevent you from seeing what they see – prevent you from seeing who you really are? It is also the limiting beliefs that you have unconsciously picked up, which prevent you from being all those things. Therefore other people get the best of you and you are left wanting.

If you think about the people who like and love you, and how they can light up at the mere sight of you, you might well start to become more curious about what it is that they see that maybe you don't.

Your 'ness' is all aspects of you, which shine through when you are fully present. Some of you will be aware of what it is and others may have no idea. We will all have experienced both perspectives, the better we know and accept ourselves fully the more we see.

Have you ever seen a photo of you looking at someone you love or doing something that you love – a photo you didn't know was being taken? If so you will probably agree you look different? Those are the moments when your 'ness' shines through brightly. It's the GOD essence within us all, which is revealed when we are fully present, enabling the divine part to shine through. This happens to us in moments of time, which we may overlook, and it is often witnessed by strangers, more so than people who supposedly know us better. Your smile, your compassion, your humanity is a gift you probably give to many more people than you realise. It is the part of us that will never die, and was with us from the beginning. Therefore, in terms of loving and cherishing it is important and right that we learn to own it and step into the presence of it more frequently. From that place we can truly feel at one with the Universe.

I am a long time member of an online group called B School led by Life Coach Marie Forleo. As part of the initial programme I took in 2014, we had to ask friends and family for feedback about our best qualities. When I reached out to people for feedback it confirmed what I had already begun to own. Mainly the feedback was that people see me as warm, passionate and enthusiastic.

But for the longest time I could not see this and I certainly didn't give warmth or love, or with enthusiasm cheer myself on in the way I clearly did to others. However, in the four years post the Priory, that is, exactly what I have been doing. Like any good best friend, I began to cheer myself on and was already making sure the woman in the mirror was getting the very best of me too. By being this person in the mirror I was loving and cherishing those parts of me which needed help. I was realising slowly, but surely, that my most important job was to show up more and to shower those attributes towards her.

By loving and cherishing myself and being even more present, more of me was coming through. No matter what we have experienced – even depression or anxiety, the story we tell is blinkered. Yet our essence has a way of shining through, more than we know and we will be blessed, by people who see it. Loving and cherishing who you are, will mean accepting what is inherently shining through from other people's perspective. So, please do ask your close family and friends this question. Ask about 25 people; *"Please tell me what my best qualities are?"* You can then choose to own them and lean into them more. Let yourself be led towards things that will bring these qualities out in you. Your job is to love and cherish yourself for those qualities – that is what your inner-self is crying out for.

6

Our Shadow side needs to be loved too

I think this is one of the messages that the Divine is constantly trying to get us to understand and fully embrace. If you listen to the stories threaded through many spiritual texts – it will say it again and again, and yet somehow we don't think it is true for us. It's okay for people we love to have flaws – we can overlook and love them regardless but – crikey not our own. No, these we often keep hidden and we think we should never reveal these shadow parts. We often make the mistake, as I did, that we have to be the shiny parts of ourselves for other people. If you can relate to this right now, I bet it feels very uncomfortable in your body?

And all the while our shadow-self sits in the dark, her denial makes her presence all the more unpredictable. For me these shadow parts are the darker side of my best qualities. All light has a shadow and these parts of me are selfish, angry and thoughtless. By my late twenties my refusal to own the shadow parts started to play havoc with my well-being. My beloved grandfathers death in January 1998 affected me deeply. I felt totally bereft and it marked a deeply unhappy time at work and at home. I was unhappy about being me, full stop, and I was spinning out of control.

As a young married couple amongst many single friends we were beginning to struggle. I worked away a lot and I began to wonder, not for the first time, if we had made a huge mistake in getting married so young. I started to feel an emptiness that no matter what, wouldn't go away. We were partying at weekends and drinking far too much and I was totally cut off from any spiritual nourishment. My inability to communicate my feelings with my husband and those around me left me feeling numb a lot of the time. I had no idea that an old deeply limiting belief that 'I wasn't loveable' was once again playing out.

With perspective and a much better understanding of the human psyche, I realise that I was also totally misinterpreting my young husband's energy and body language so I had no idea what was going on in his mind most of the time. My unhelpful thoughts were totally unquestioned and my acting-out behaviour that followed was based purely on thoughts from deep within my subconscious and from my inner critic.

Of course my 29-year-old self knew nothing about the process of questioning your thoughts, nor did she have a clue that the Source of love was inside her. One weekend, that summer I ended up on an all-day drinking session with an old friend, who I had a crush on since my teens. With a cocktail of too much alcohol, unexpressed emotions and emptiness inside, it was a car crash waiting to happen. The result was a drunken kiss. I acted like a 17-year-old, the realities of being a married woman felt far away. It was as if I had simply travelled back in time. Thankfully the weirdest thing happened, with the potential of things going physically further I came too, and became fully present. I no longer felt 17 and I became a sober, wiser woman not remotely interested in behaving like a 17-year- old and that was that. It was as if I had just woken up from a foggy 18 months.

As we chatted the next day about what had happened and the horror and shame set in, I remember him saying; *"I think this is your cry for help Bernie"*. It has been one of the hardest things for me to learn, to ask for help. All those years later as I lay on my bed in the Priory the only words GOD spoke to me were *"Call out for help call out for help now"*. Help was on its way, back then too.

This event caused me so much shame and remorse for over ten years and became my darkest secret. If I could take back what I did, because of the pain it caused, I would. But as I look back I realise I wouldn't be who I am today if I hadn't had to do the forgiveness and soul searching that I believed was purely because of this incident. GOD had heard my cry for help and I was on my own long road to awakening to the truth of who I was. In my life changing moment in 2010 I could honestly say that everything that had happened to me in my life, had happened for me.

But back then; this low point marked a turning point in my marriage. I realised I didn't want things to end at all and I realised how much I really loved my husband. I opened up about how unhappy I had been and we saw that we had both simply been feeling unseen and unloved by one other. I was, however, too afraid to tell him what had happened. I had form (from our college days) and I was sure he would leave me, and all our friends would say; "we knew it wouldn't last". So I kept the secret locked from him for ten years – costing us both dearly. Secrets affect how we feel inside and are reflected out into the world. This is often, misinterpreted by other people as being about them. The scenarios that were affected by my internal shame are too many to mention, it was like a dark shadow that followed me everywhere. It would become dormant for a while but then something would happen to trigger the feeling of shame, and I feared GOD would punish me for what I had done.

Inevitably my relationship with my friend changed forever and it affected relationships everywhere I turned. My shameful secret became buried deeper inside me and the dark thoughts that came with it affected my behaviour. I was a good Catholic girl and Catholic guilt is a dark force of nature!

Within four months I felt a physical wreck. I remember with my husband's insistence going to the doctor. The lovely almost-to-retire doctor warned me that stress was not something to take lightly and he strongly recommended I make some changes. I said nothing about my personal life. Work, was by now, incredibly stressful and this, too, was added into the mix.

I had become a senior manager with a huge geographical region and my job just wasn't fun any more. If someone, had asked me my 'why?' back then, I doubt I would have been able, to give a great answer. During this time, I really didn't know how to function properly at times and it was a colleague, who ironically, I was finding challenging who recommended I sought out a counsellor.

This was my pattern. To my husband I shared, the stress was due to my relationship with my colleague, and to my colleagues I shared, it was my relationship with my boss which was causing me stress. I couldn't be honest about the root cause because at the very root of it, was my belief that I wasn't loveable. Yet in that moment I believed the cause was my shame.

The counselling organisation I finally went to was part of the Christian church. It helped to open up, as I had not done so, for the longest time. After a couple of sessions I admitted to the kissing incident and I was told I had committed adultery. I was devastated and heart broken. It was so so painful to own this darkness but at least now someone knew and yes GOD knew. Now I had to atone, and if my marriage was going to survive I was going to have to accept this dark part of me. I stopped going to the sessions and I was done with GOD for good. I was going to have to live with this as best I could. I decided to put it all behind me and move on. I had kept secrets before, so I could live with this one – another skeleton would simply move into my closet.

Now I can see, that accepting this part of me caused a shift. I started to take care of myself better. I gradually regained trust in myself, and my relationship with my husband and colleagues at work improved. More of me was present and I felt more stable in myself as the months went on. But I also noticed that I was terrified of getting too happy. In my mind GOD knew what I was, so happiness was not going to be something I fully deserved. I was convinced if I became too happy something terrible would happen – that would be my punishment.

We started trying for a baby and I did my best to dismiss the inner voice telling me I would never get pregnant. I believed, to want a child and now not get one, would be my punishment. So when, in September 2000, I discovered I was pregnant it felt like a miracle had occurred. I knew this child had been conceived out of total love and a small part of me began to hope that maybe, just maybe, things were not so black-and-white.

We are the light and the dark – we are the everything and yet, despite what we might believe, we are loved regardless. The parts of us labelled as dark are to do with our unique gifts.

Source sees all parts of us and loves us anyway and I felt that love so deeply in the moment I discovered I was pregnant. Having stepped into, and owned my shadows I now realise I was rediscovering my connection to GOD. She wants us all to experience the same viewpoint. She wants us to be compassionate and understanding to ourselves. That is what love does. Yet to experience it, we need to be willing to step into the shadow again and again. I don't think we can even begin the journey to self-love without the essential travelling companion of self- forgiveness. Without forgiving myself, how could I have even dared to believe that I was loveable and dare I did, because with this pregnancy the power of forgiveness was already underway.

As a movie fan I notice this subject pops up in films all the time. The darker elements of us are played out as the evil dark forces. The witch in the 'Wizard of Oz', Darth Vader in 'Star Wars', The Dark One in 'Once Upon a Time'. Our reaction to these dark characters is very important – the more we abhor them and reject them, the more we are in denial of our own shadow side. Time and time again we see these characters, finally remembering their light – by being brave to no longer be afraid of their dark, they are no longer afraid of their own light. My beautiful daughter owning her light and coming into my world helped me to reclaim mine.

That is what we have to do within ourselves. We need to be brave and courageous and step into our light so that we can then shine that light on the darkness of our own individual human selves. Our mess-ups, our shame, our supposed inadequacies, our hurts, so that the parts of us stuck in the dark can come home into the true lightness of who we are.

It is never done through judgement, only through courage, acceptance, love and understanding.

My own experience has shown me that the very people we meet in our lives who we dislike, criticise internally or find abhorrent represent parts of ourselves that we have rejected. Parts we deplore that we have shoved into our shadow. These people are actually the messengers, here to help us. Once we acknowledge that and do the internal healing work of loving another hidden aspect of our selves these same individuals seem to change before our eyes. As we love and accept that part of ourselves more of their light is revealed to us at the same time.

Being, by nature, a nosey person I have observed many people in my life. People watching as a passion, was for a reason after all! Those that I see living with the most freedom and the most joy are without doubt those that own their humanity, their shadow and their light. They didn't feel the need to hide their flaws. Somehow they know 'being human' is okay. They are not hiding parts of themselves away. That is their true power and harnessing it, allows for eternal lightness.

Make peace with who you are

This is such an important step in the self-healing, self-love journey. Acceptance of all that we are, our past choices, our so-called mistakes, our shames, our shadows, how we look and how we see the world. Making peace with the childhood experiences, which have made us who we are today, is essential. From this peaceful place, real miracles can happen.

Fully making peace with who I was, on that day in 2010, led me back to the Divinity within me. The memory is still so incredible it fills me with joy every time I revisit it. Divinity I was always taught resided outside of me, yet was actually deep inside me. This is where we 'sin', the meaning of which is really to 'miss the mark'. Being me was always enough, always had been, but I only discovered that, once I made peace with all that I wasn't and embraced all that I was.

Sometimes I am so aware of this Divinity, I feel as if I am, literally, in heaven. I don't believe we come here, to earn a way to heaven by making peace with God. We discover that we never left when we make peace with ourselves.

At other times I can see how I have jumped back into small battles with myself and things feel far from heavenly. This lasts a much shorter time than it used to, but it's a reminder that peace is something, which needs to be maintained. We only have to look at the world stage to see how peace can be shattered all too easily. If we don't invest in peaceful behaviour towards ourselves, if we ignore the darker elements and the personal power we all weld, things can get messy all over again.

If we look at our mirrors and by that I mean, all that is reflected back to us from the world. If we judge any of it, peace has been broken. Somewhere a battle, no matter how small, is underway. I think it is because we are often in denial of our flaws, because to admit to having them or reveal them would mean that those we love might turn against us. Subconsciously we seek perfection from all around us. Because we can't bear our own imperfections, we need to make peace with all parts hiding in our subconscious.

Once we make peace with our imperfections with our humanity, only then can we see perfection in those around us.

In the past, as I navigated my way through different social groups, I struggled with many parts of me. I remember this starting as early as four-years-old. My shyness, my uncertainty, my intelligence, my religion, my nationality, my social class, my weight, my accent, my skin colour, my occupation, my ambition, my eating choices, my music choices, my hair colour, complexion, chest size, thigh size, sense of humour, sense of seriousness, even my spirituality. I could go on – it's an endless list.

I am now choosing to trust that the Universal Source doesn't get it wrong in our make up. I now believe that we have all been uniquely created for a certain reason and that the parts of us which seem different are actually necessary for our time here to be the most effective.

Think of any person in history who has done something you truly admire or any close friend or relative who made a massive positive impact on you. Chances are they understood that embracing all of who they were – the odd sticky out bits, was the magical ingredient in their lives. The amount of energy we waste when we try to change what we think is flawed is one of the human tragedies. Yet we all probably, to a certain degree, have to experience this, even if it causes us the most suffering. From that suffering we have the opportunity to remember who we truly are. In an attempt to blend-in and make ourselves small we are missing the magical opportunity that awaits us on the other side, of embracing exactly all of who we are. In each and every turn, I was often the total opposite of being at peace with who I was. Yet now, I have faith that each and every one of those elements is needed. These elements were essential and still are essential for how I am meant to show up in this world.

Sure they are different from people whom I admire, more similar than I want to admit from people whom I judge. In both cases of comparison I am at war with who I am and that's a war where no one leaves alive. I think we are here to wake up to a reality. The reality that the peace is within us, and always was, it was never about someone else's actions or way of showing up.

It's exhausting and depleting, to say the least, to be in a constant state of war with who we fundamentally are.

None of these things can ever define us. This is not what this experience is about, we are much more complex. Our past choices are complicated, but our time here as spiritual beings on a human journey and all that comes with it, is temporary – fighting all the way through it is the madness.

The moment we stop fighting with 'the character' we get to experience this sooner, we harness the skills and superpowers that come with it. Trying to be like someone else and rejecting any part of ourselves negates the gifts that only we have individually.

So whether it's your skin colour, hair colour, accent, way of dressing, physic ability, introvert or extrovert nature, sensitivity, sense of humour, sexual preferences or history, interests or perspective, cultural and religious or non religious perspectives. The list will be endless, but there will be something obviously different about you. Embrace it, especially if it feels at odds to those around you. There is a reason you experience life a certain way – it has clues and guidance, mystery and magic weaved through it. And it is for all of our benefits, that you express fully, who you truly are and the perspective you truly have.

Don't wish your oddities away– get wholeheartedly curious about them – and you just might see, that understanding these unique seeds will make all the difference. Only we can call 'time for peace' and making peace with all parts of who we are, is the only guarantee to lasting peace.

8

No one wins when you dim your light

Dimming our light is part of the human experience – our need to have faith in our world is paramount. At the first sign of something feeling off, we think we must have done something wrong and this means we take on the task of adapting and changing our behaviour. It's in tiny things at first but in this process we stop being ourselves and start doing what we think other people want or need us to do.

For me, I look back and see that my light started to dim at the age of three. My Mum had just given birth and this, of course, should have been a joyous occasion. However, even as little as three, I sensed something was off – a dark cloud seemed to enter the household. The reason was that one of the two babies mum was expecting had died at birth. So the twins didn't come home, as no doubt, my older brothers and sister had expected. My new little brother had to make his journey home alone. As the former baby of the house I was oblivious to this. All I knew, was my once happy mummy, seemed to have a sadness about her. Without anyone realising it, I thought maybe I had done something wrong. This is not unique to me. It's what all small children who are sensitive do, when things shift away from the energy of pure love we feel we must be doing something wrong. As young as three-years-old I felt something else was going on. I could feel a sadness, and although I didn't understand it I felt it and absorbed it.

I remember sitting in row, on the bed, with my three older siblings. We are three, four, five and six-years-old consecutively. Someone has put us there and we have been told to be quiet, something we have never experienced before. I remember having a toy with me – my favourite toy – a musical mini organ with little muppet-like heads that make sounds when you tap the keyboard. As it's the only toy in the room my two older brothers start to play with it. I don't like how they are being so rough with it and I start to cry, trying to get it off them. Only to be told; *"You're such a cry baby."* As the youngest being called a cry-baby is the ultimate put down and I am not a baby! My stubbornness kicks in, I make the tears stop and all I feel is numbness. There the memory stops – but I was a baby who really wanted to cry and cry and cry, because my brothers were never normally mean so I must have done something wrong.

My three-year-old self – the one who needed to cry because her beautiful world now seemed so horrible, the one who needed a loving presence to swoop down and make her and her siblings all feel safe and loved. That moment stayed with me and with a belief that 'no-one loves me'. I didn't make a fuss, I didn't tell tales, I didn't seek out the comfort from my Mummy, and I didn't get to question that ridiculous thought to ensure it had no power over me. It became the dark seed that would grow inside me. This thought would play out in school, in college, in work – all unconsciously but feeding the darkness as it did.

What I didn't realise, of course, that I was feeling all of my beautiful Mum's grief. The grief over losing a child had also triggered the grief she had buried nine years earlier over losing her own mother whilst she herself, was really still a child at only sixteen-years-old. It was years later she opened up to me and told me what she was dealing with. We both felt very alone at that time, it seems.

Roll forward to 2010 when all things shifted into place. I understood my life in a whole new gorgeous way but I still didn't realise this belief was locked away. It was still driving my behaviour without me realising it. This is the reason we need to release and heal old subconscious beliefs. It's like computer programming, we have to remove the glitches and ensure that its capacity isn't limiting.

As my quest for healing continued I sought out an energy healer. During an energy healing session with my coach Melody Fletcher I had a beautiful healing experience, which brought me back to the time my little sister had died. And by doing so and being so gentle with my three-year-old self I started to release this old outdated belief. This limiting belief stored deep in my subconscious would be the root cause for many of my insecurities that created shame and suffering. To me this sums up so much of what happens to all humans in childhood.

Did you know that one of the most common human beliefs responsible for much of our suffering is the lie, that we are not loveable and that, we have been abandoned by our Source of Love. I promise you, that you are not and have never been abandoned. The truth is, Source never left you, not even for a moment.

Dr Bruce Lipton explains that at a young age the mind is operating in the Theta state associated with wild imagination and hypnosis. We are literally sponges up to about the age of seven or eight. There are as many neural pathways in our brain, as there are stars in the universe, and yet we use so few of them. One of the reasons for this is perhaps, the fact that we form two neural pathways in our brains at the same time. This can cause us to become stuck in the past, returning to the same neural pathways again and again, leaving many unexplored. In the scenario with my siblings my three-year-old self simply shoved away a very vivid double meaning.

Amazingly sometime ago I found this quote on the internet which sums up the kind of double message hastily stored away by my amazing pathways during that painful time; "*Being left out is horrible, but you can't say anything without feeling jealous or like a cry-baby and no one loves a cry-baby*"

And with every unquestioned belief, little or big, our ability to feel the internal illumination that is so present in babies – as the whole beings we are – gradually decreases. Little incidents misunderstood cause us to dim our light again and again. We are all powerful beings yet we are often oblivious to this. We simply do not realise that we are even dimming our light, and if we dim our light, other people around us dim their lights too.

Fortunately it is not happening to us all at the same time – we will be surrounded by other beings of light at different stages of the journey to reawaken. And of course have the joy of fully present beings to help us in the form of babies, animals, and other earth angels – but none of them can make our light illuminate – that is, of course, an inside job. Their role is to, through example, show us how it can be done so that we remember for ourselves. They, by knowing their light, reflect that back to us and gradually we begin to awaken one by one – all in our own good time.

If you are reading this and thinking I know this, I am awake, but if only my partner, parents, friends or colleagues could wake up then things would be great. I'm afraid you are simply, believing another illusion. We are all on our own human journey and we all have the capacity to see all beings as whole and complete without anyone changing but ourselves.

Let's continue to journey on with the messages from the doodles and see if we can shine a light on some of the misunderstandings that have kept us from illuminating our own darkness and reclaim the parts of us that we really do need to shine.

9

Look in the mirror and smile at who you see

In the fairy tale world of the Netflix series *'Once upon a Time'*, the enchanted mirror of Snow White's step-mother the Wicked Queen, is her constant go to. The Queen uses it to appease her deep and painful insecurities and in the modern world, because of this long established fairytale, a mirror to this day brings up feelings of both vanity and shallowness.

I can sympathise with the Queen's frequent need for reassurance. As a teenager I would pass a mirror hung on one of the school walls by a cloakroom, almost daily, and just like the Queen I couldn't resist looking into it. Every time I did, I whispered a prayer – please make me look the most beautiful I can be, please make me seem more beautiful today.

In the fairytale, the mirror is actually the home of someone imprisoned, someone who was enchanted by the Queen's external beauty. Looking back I can see that, I too, was the prisoner in the mirror, mesmerised by external beauty and feeling totally bereft of it.

Yet what if mirrors truly are magical portals? Through which you can see your inner wise self – a portal where you could connect eye-to-eye with your Divinity.

When children below the age of two look in the mirror they always reach out to it – as if they see someone else. For years psychologists have said it is because they have yet to develop a sense of self and it is usually only from 18 months onwards that this occurs, and they can only then see themselves. You can test this throughout their second year by putting a large red dot of lipstick on their head and standing them in front of the mirror from time-to-time. Initially they will always instinctively reach into the mirror – wanting to connect to the person they see there. They will smile and laugh at each other. It's a beautiful thing to witness. But then one day they will just suddenly stop reaching into the mirror and smiling at who they see. Instead they will put their hands up to their forehead and wipe off the lipstick – self awareness and self consciousness has begun. This magical portal now seems closed. I remember doing this with both my children and feeling a little saddened on both occasions, when the magic seemed to stop.

But what if up to that point they have been connecting with Source? Their inner wise self, because in reality, they are still fully aware of the connection – fully conscious and in the bubble of love. No wonder they laugh and smile.

What if we can all reconnect to Source via this magical portal?

I'll admit I was one or two tequilas down when I stepped into the toilets on board the river boat on a Christmas night out. It was the late 90s and I was at the height of my career and whilst very happy in my relationship once more I was deeply unhappy at work. Two months before, I had spent time in the Caribbean with some new friends and the contrast to how I felt now, labelled as, 'one of the management' at this team gathering was horrible. I felt so uncomfortable with my colleagues and those on my team. I felt I really needed to be alone for a few minutes, fearing that my face would give me away. I had no idea that I was practically a pro at wearing a mask.

When I looked into the mirror and let the mask fall away for those precious moments just as I might have done as a tiny child. I looked directly into the eyes of another. In that moment I know I saw my inner wise self. I remember laughing and engaging with her and feeling for the longest time a truth, she really loves me. It was a sweet, sweet reunion and it still makes me emotional to think of it today.

The smile she gave me was incredible – for a moment all pain dissolved – pain caused by my own insecurities, and momentarily I felt free, free to finally be me.

That was 20 years ago and while it lasted only a few minutes, it was a pivotal moment in my life. Within two years I had shifted into a much healthier mindset and was months away from becoming a mother for the first time, finally leaving behind the life I had never actually wanted. I had re-established the connection and from here on in my inner wisdom was able to lead the way. She would lead me to that homecoming in the Priory ten years later. Today, as I verge ever closer to entering another new decade, I have in the process of writing this book had the opportunity to take counsel from her many times. I simply take a deep breath, and I am able to see her with my own eyes in the mirror. These words always help me and if you want to take a leap into your own portal then maybe it's time to take a fresh look into a mirror too.

Aided by these words (a little lyrical verse of song that I came up with a few years ago) reconnect with your very own inner wise self:

Coming Home.

"Look in the mirror
Smile at who you see
tell the whole world
You're happy to be me

Look in the mirror
Smile at who you see
tell the whole world
and set yourself free!!

Tell the whole world
You're happy to be me!"

We all need to heal the inner child

Shortly after my awakening, I realised that old fears were coming back with a vengeance. Whilst staying at the Priory, I was disproportionately upset by male angry voices and I seemed to become like a small child, when dealing with a blunt direct comment. Surely this was something I could, and needed to address? I got really curious, and I got busy.

I came to understand, through my own investigation, that my inner child had many unresolved issues, and she really needed to heal. It was this inner child that had been paralysed by secrets.

As the clues became apparent, over the next year or so, I set to work to heal. I sought out a picture of my four-year-old self and whereas once before I had looked at this same photo critically, seeing nothing but my chubby face, I now saw a child beautifully open and loving. This picture goes onto my vision board every time I redo it, keeping her front and at the centre of my self-loving journey.

In order to heal her wounds I began to speak to myself as I would a four-year-old child. I encouraged and coaxed myself so compassionately when I messed up and I kept a picture of my four-year-old self close to hand. The healing was profound and over time has been miraculous.

I ask all my clients to bring a picture of themselves at this age to our earliest possible session. I also ask that they keep it where they can see it daily. I encourage them to speak to themselves with the love, compassion and gentleness that they would to a four-year-old child who, was upset or nervous. The experience of doing this for me has been massive and from the feedback from my clients, it seems to have been life changing for them too.

Search out a photo of your three or four-year-old self. Notice how you react to it, how you judge her or him and then make a commitment to speak to yourself in this newly compassionate way and keep her or him visible. After a few weeks you will feel differently about yourself, about your inner child and you will be able to show up more as the present adult you are, but with the open heart of a young child – even in scary or tricky situations.

10

Connect with the teacher inside you

Depending on our own personal experiences with teachers this may, at first, bring up different emotions for you. Most of us have been massively, affected by teachers in our educational lifetime and this was the case for me. Generally we have one or two teachers who stand out and provided a memorable positive learning experience. My Primary 1 and Primary 5 teachers are the ones I recall. They are I feel, the teachers who understood me and, therefore, knew how to get the best out of me. In fact they seemed to know how to get the most out of everyone in the class. I remember my P5 teacher with great affection. Her name was Una McGinn. I think it's safe to say we all adored her. Sadly, she left after only a year and it felt like she really did leave a big hole in our lives. Most of us muddled through, however one of the girls in my class went from showing huge potential to losing all interest in her education. Her educational relapse from top of the class to bottom stayed with me – all that lost potential. I used to wonder how things might have been different for her, if she had realised the potential the teacher saw in her and had gone on to Grammar School as had looked very likely in that year.

What if the teacher we are meant to connect with is the one deep inside of us? The one who will never leave and the one who will guide us to realise our full potential?

I now believe she is there and has been there all the time. My P5 teacher was actually a glimpse of what lay inside me.

In my coaching work I have guided many people to connect with that inner wisdom and the thing which struck me as I looked at this doodle was the tone of voice that is the inner wisdom – our very own inner teacher – is a lot like the tone of voice my P5 teacher used. Encouraging, loving, patient, and sometimes firm but, always full of love. My inner wisdom also reminds me a lot of my P1 teacher's warm, loving, gentle presence, which saw us all, as bright shining stars.

How do we connect with that inner teacher on a day to day basis?

Firstly we have to be still and in doing so we connect with our breath and from that space we can breathe deeply. So much of our time is spent flitting from one online stimulant to another, as we search for advice from Google or other sources. Our own wisdom locked deep inside us is often ignored. What if, as well as relying on Google we connect to the stillness inside? Ask the questions and wait for the guidance.

Questions any great teacher will ask us are; *"What seems to be the problem, what are you afraid of?"* Because it's okay to be scared and uncertain and maybe what you are afraid of, isn't actually true. Look at this in a different way – what do you feel is the next best move? Then maybe what could you do next? What in all of this feels right to you? You can do this!

Simply by asking ourselves these questions by assuming the role of the teacher within, we will find our way forward – connecting and being the teacher hand-in-hand. By adapting the tone of voice of our favourite teacher we will feel safe to experiment, to take that step. Who knows where that will lead us?

Take a few moments to remember your favourite teacher, and next time, you feel stuck speak to yourself in their tone of voice. Ask yourself the questions that amazing teacher would have asked, and be ready to take action – one step after another.

11

What other people think of you is none of your business

I remember vividly the first time I heard these words. It was about week three into my stay at the Priory and I was spending a couple of hours out in 'the real world' in Southside Glasgow with one of the staff members. She was to be one of my early spiritual guides in this new phase of my human existence.

We were sitting having a cup of tea in a little café and were chatting about me going home. I said something along the lines of; *"people will think I'm a flake"* and she looked me straight in the eye and said something which has stayed with me almost as a protective super-power cloak.

"Bernie what other people think of you is none of your business."

I remember initially feeling a bit told off by her words because in my past I had probably been told off because of my nosiness, with similar words; *"That's none of your business."* So my initial reaction was interesting; *"what do you mean it's none of my business of course it is"*. But she just smiled and shook her head; *"No it's not."*

Within a few seconds something started to click and when she explained further I began to experience a new sensation. It was like another epiphany and the next feeling was one of relief. It was as if

I had just been given permission to drop a massive sack that I had permanently been carrying on my back.

"Hold on" I said; "*You mean it's actually none of my business – I don't have to give it the amount of thought that I do, I don't have to be concerned about what I think other people's reactions to me are – so I don't have to waste any of my time and energy wondering about what they think of me. It's really none of my business? It's really not my concern, nothing to do with me. It's their business – not mine – I can just get on with living my life*". "Yes" she said smiling, and suddenly my smile grew to match.

She was right. You simply can't know or control other people's thoughts – it's a fool's game to try to, and it's exhausting. I was so exhausted from 41 years of worrying about what other people thought of me. I gave it way too much energy, so had no energy left to be. No wonder I felt uncreative.

How about you – how does this statement make you feel? Just tell yourself now; "*what other people think of you is none of your business.*"

How would you dress, walk, talk throughout your day? How would it change how you behaved around other people? How would it affect your morning if you waved to someone you know but they didn't wave back or you? Or smiled at someone but got little response? These used to send me into a tailspin; "*What have I done to upset them I wonder*", or I would feel she or he clearly doesn't like me.

People have far more to think about in their lives and sometimes they are just lost in thoughts that they don't notice the wave or the smile. They may just have had a row with their partner or, be worrying about money. They are in thought somewhere, it will rarely if ever, be about you.

Instead of spending time wondering or worrying about what other people think of you, say to your inner critic; "*It's none of my business we are in someone else's business here and let it go.*"

Consider these scenarios. You say no to someone you usually always say yes to because the old thought was; "I want their approval". Now you know it's none of your business – you can just say no – job done.

You need to be open about the part of you that has messed up. But you are so afraid of what other people think of you, so you repress it. This, of course, could lead to a bigger more complicated mess. Now you know it's none of your business what others think and you can connect to something stronger inside. You can step forward, own the mess and the situation is resolved far quicker.

You can reply to emails when ready, without apology instead of previously breaking your neck to reply instantly in case the sender thinks you are rude. Why the change? Because what other people think of you is none of your business.

You wave to someone but they don't wave back. Now instead of fretting you let it go, send them love. You repeat the words; *"It's none of my business"* and get on with being present in your day.

You share something you have created in this world to a larger audience and you find your work feels lighter and more honest. Why? Because, once again, you have remembered; *"what other people think of you is none of your business."*

Breath deeply, love fiercely, Forgive all

Raised as a Roman Catholic, never far from my ears was the word 'forgiveness', and sayings such as 'God forgive you' or, more morosely, 'I'll never forgive myself' or 'I'll never forgive you'. These words flavoured my existence growing up. Weekly, at Mass on a Sunday, we would ask for forgiveness, born as sinners, constantly needing to repent. This comes from a belief that we are born of sin, which, if I'm honest, always bothered me. I have experienced real beauty in that faith but some of these unquestioned beliefs need, I think, to be questioned, as could our relationship with forgiveness. I feel this to be true for all religions, which have a faith based on the unquestioned belief that we are born of sin, with a definition of sin as a negative. Sin, originally a Latin word, actually refers to a word used in archery terms and means 'to miss the mark'.

In 2005 we moved, as a family, from the village outside Glasgow to North Berwick to live our dream life by the sea. But after a couple of years, my stress levels started to rise again. I was nearly 39 and we had two amazing children, as our son followed two years after our daughter.

I thought I had made peace with my past and had moved on. But as our quality of life rose, and I dared to be happy, so too did my stress levels. I began to get chest pains and immediately recognised the pains in my chest from my late twenties. What could I be stressed about now though? We lived in a beautiful seaside town in a beautiful house with two gorgeous children. I knew I loved my husband. Despite being a regular runner this stress feeling kept coming back, it was as if I couldn't outrun the feeling. I sought more counselling. I knew I needed to open up, but felt it had to be someone who didn't know my husband. I couldn't bear the thought of anyone I knew being burdened by something that I wouldn't tell him. This experience proved very powerful for me. I met several times with an amazing Canadian woman, who was so full of love and compassion, and I felt I was ready for the next level of energy healing. I say, ready for, because when I work with people as an energy coach, there has to be a state of readiness for me to be the right person. There has to be foundational inner work before they are able to connect deeper to the love inside them. With her help I was able to make the decision to forgive myself, and those that I felt had hurt me in my past with their own suffering. She was the person who really helped me see that forgiveness is an inside job. My chest pains disappeared and I felt I could go on from here alone. She had a deep faith, it seemed different from other religious people I had met and yet familiar too. Even so, I wanted nothing to do with any religion, but her compassion and sincerity did leave a lasting impression. Looking back, I can see these were all steps towards a loving relationship with myself. What held me back from leaning on GOD more was, I was sure I would have to change into somebody else by letting parts of me go – the opposite turned out to be my truth. I would return to GOD only when I loved, cherished and forgave all of me and let go of the story that had kept me in the dark.

Brené Brown, whose work I discovered six months after I left the Priory was one of the first people I heard talking publicly about shame. Her Ted Talk in 2011 captivated me. She went onto to write about vulnerability and shame in her book 'Daring Greatly'. One of the keys to releasing yourself from shame, is forgiveness, I was now my own proof of that. You absolutely have to forgive yourself for whatever it is, and you will only realise that this is something you need to heal, through the triggers you experience in your daily life.

When triggers occur, as they must if we are to evolve, we have a choice. We can either react and buy into the illusion or question our thoughts. Through this process, (the one I still use, is 'The Work' by Byron Katie) you are able to look at the root of the pain, feel it and then let it go. Only when this happens does a powerful shift occur.

This is something I help my clients with a lot. This is the power of coaching. I have had to forgive myself for many things, to get to where I am on my coaching journey. And yes more comes up as I go along, and yes, again looking inside – well it's sometimes really hard! It's always easier to look at someone else's problems. Looking at our own is painful and sometimes ugly but I promise you, when you do and the healing occurs, the feeling is amazing.

Only when you stop putting yourself into situations, which will hurt you, will the forgiveness not be necessary, and this really requires us all to listen to our inner wisdom, our precious intuition as we move through life.

I do believe this makes all the difference. It's when we don't hear or listen to our feelings or intuition that we cause ourselves hurt.

So, if like me, you have made human choices that you need to forgive yourself for, please do so now. You can't change the past or control the future but trust me you were born of pure love and, if like me, somewhere along the way you have forgotten this, conditioned by other's conditioning – I promise you it's not your fault. The good news is, I very much have hope in my heart that once we really learn to question our thoughts in the present moment, and forgive ourselves for the things in our past, the old pattern of behaviour is dissolved. We will have successfully peeled off another layer that covers our pure wholeness.

Source loves you unconditionally – no forgiveness is necessary. You can go to confessions, you can ask for forgiveness, but to really awaken the GOD in you, you have to start loving yourself unconditionally and be the one that truly forgives you. Why? Because, you are the Source – the power of forgiveness lies in you.

Forgiveness exercise:

This exercise and the following extract has been taken from the book; '*Tapping the Power Within*' by Iyanla Vanzant.

The ironic thing about forgiveness, the truth about it, is that in all matters of the heart, it is ultimately ourselves we have to forgive the most. This is necessary, because if we do not forgive, the person we end up hurting the most is our self. To forgive ourselves, and another is very powerful and it is something we will have to revisit many times. This has been true for me. This exercise may highlight your resistance to forgive and so, if you find yourself skipping a day please start right back at the beginning. If this proves too difficult, please be as compassionate with yourself as possible. Because it will just mean a stubborn reluctance to let go and, like you would with a small child, gently coax yourself back and start again.

"*If you are not receiving good things in your life, you need to forgive. If you are not giving freely and feeling good about it, you need to forgive. If there is anyone about whom you have painful or negative memories you need to forgive. If you are feeling lonely desperate and confused you have to forgive. Forgiveness is the spiritual laxative that purges the mind, the heart, the spirit.*"

You can now see how this will be ongoing! This is a forgiveness detox as offered also in the text '*The Course of Miracles*'. It is a powerful and effective tool for releasing past hurts, ones we remember and those that we don't. It will require 20 minutes in the morning before noon, and 20 minutes at night. You will also need a new notebook.

Firstly, choose a time in the morning when you will not be disturbed by anyone and on a clean page in the notebook number 1-35 with a line between.

On each line write this:

"I (your name) forgive (a person you blame) totally and unconditionally."

It is important that you do not pick and choose the names just let them come, any name that pops into your head. This is not a logical exercise but an emotional one. You may feel drawn to write the same name more than once and that is okay but do try to write 35 different experiences.

Once you have these lines, take five or six deep breaths and close the book. Then go about your day. At bedtime, again making sure you are not disturbed, repeat the exercise. But this time write this sentence:

"I (your name) forgive myself totally and unconditionally. I am free to move onto wholeness and completeness"

This is important. You may not know the reason why you have to forgive – it doesn't matter, as your essence, your inner wisdom, will know the reason. Just allow the names and thoughts to flow, and the forgiveness to flow. We are energetic beings and so this is energy healing work, not logically explainable but massively powerful.

Do this exercise for seven mornings and seven evenings with no interruptions if you miss a day start back at day one.

Here is another extract from Iyanla's book I love;

"Forgiveness is a powerful act of self love and self discovery. Forgiveness does not erase the memory of an experience; it neutralises the impact. The deepest healing occurs when you can forgive what you have told yourself about someone else. Forgiveness is a state of being that supports the unfolding of your authentic self"

Of course, forgiveness is not easy and this does not mean you have to forget. But it is the only way to cleanse your heart so you are more in alignment with who you truly are. Transforming the blame into a blessing and the hurt into a healing. Some of the names will also surprise you. Little things forgotten from childhood could be the reason and it is just as important to forgive even without knowing why. It is all for our spiritual evolution. Don't be surprised if you are suddenly contacted by or bump into someone on your list. Pay attention to how you feel and react. If you have totally forgiven them you will experience a new sense of freedom.

Doing this exercise alone is a huge act of self-love. It's giving yourself permission to be free once more – so go towards it with love and light, and with the knowledge that in doing so you are a brave and courageous beacon of light.

Love and forgive
all parts of you

In 2018, I was part of a group invited to stay in Villa Casa Fuzetta in Olhao, Portugal. As part of a food walking tour led by the amazing Joana from Eating Algarve, we learned about the history of Portuguese food as we munched our way along. Throughout the day as Joana spoke she repeated this line several times; *"We were invaded and we were invaders and our food represents that now"*

Throughout the first century the Spanish, Africans and Balkans invaded Portugal one-by-one and as they did, they brought their food ideas and their traditions. When the Portuguese invaded other countries they brought their own influences to those countries. What is now evident in Portuguese food and their attitudes is the huge mixture of all of these elements.

Before you think I've switched to writing a food book let's take a look at how this thought comes to play in this context;

"We were invaded and we were invaders. Love and forgive all parts of you."

When I chatted to Joana, later that evening, I asked her about the acceptance of invader as well as invaded. She smiled and nodded in agreement; *"Yes maybe we have accepted all of our parts and we are much more in balance now, because of that."*

One of the things that stood out for me, amongst the Portuguese I spent time with, was their overall and balanced friendliness. Their acceptance of the invader and invaded identity must surely be a contributing factor. Through their long history of evolution and political unrest, somehow they have been able to forgive all parts, all sides, and the result being, they live as balanced people. They are in tune with themselves and a real sense of balance and emotional strength is evident. The energy of the people I met was very loving and friendly. I now felt sure I knew why.

In Irish and Scottish history, I often hear about invasion but have not yet heard us describing ourselves as invaders. Based on the Spanish history timeline, our guide referred to, I am sure both Irish and Scottish people need to own the role of invader too.

Maybe a key element to the healing and peace we all seek, lies in our acceptance of our national history over the centuries, our family history and our personal history too? By taking responsibility and owning all parts of the invader and the invaded, we can lean into loving and forgiving all of them equally.

Hand over your
fear to me

In the summer of 2009 we headed off for a family five-week trip of a lifetime, to California and Costa Rica. A few months earlier my husband had been made redundant and we took the opportunity to take this extended trip before he started to look for more work. His work had been very stressful and he was away a lot, so I felt sure this was going to be a positive experience, but I was really struggling with my demons, once again, so I was very distracted in the lead up to our departure.

My happiness limit was being pushed once more, and I couldn't help but notice that a pattern emerged before all our holidays. Something always seemed to go physically wrong with me. This time bang on form, I developed toothache at the last minute. However, armed with painkillers and a new filling, off we flew.

Although my toothache came too, and even with all the amazing things going on, I was having to face one of my biggest fears – loosing my teeth. My mother and father both lost many of their teeth at a pretty young age, and I had always been afraid of this happening to me. The tooth in question already had a crown, so it was going to mean a gap on my right side. This filled me with horror. My teeth have always been my vanity area and I was so terrified of loosing a tooth and my big toothy smile. But, also, I did not want to spoil this amazing trip.

We visited Yosemite for a few days, as planned, with the hope my tooth would settle down. But of course you can't outrun the inevitable. And a few days later whilst my husband and the kids visited Monterey Aquarium, I took a cab to have my tooth extracted. It's a funny thing fear, it literally stops when you are in the middle of the very thing you have feared. As soon as you accept the inevitable, the fear disappears.

I remember sitting outside the dentist afterwards and feeling really emotional when my family pulled up to collect me. My whole world was in that car, and I had chosen for the longest time, fear over faith. This was what choosing faith over fear looked like.

As the tooth settled, we journeyed further down the pacific coast but now my husband seemed to become easily agitated, especially when we took the kids out to restaurants or we were around lots of people in parks. Eventually I asked him what was going on. He said; *"It's just this book I'm reading you'll like it and I don't want to spoil it for you by telling you too much about it."*

On our way to Costa Rica, he started to relax, and as I began reading the book it became clear. The book was about a child being abducted and the serial killer's calling card was a ladybird. Everywhere he had turned in California there were pictures or banners shaped like ladybirds. The irony! But again I thought the same old thought; *"I'm not loveable I'm not loveable"* when he was actually having distressing thoughts that were nothing about me. Yet I felt them anyway, and made them all about me.

As I read, it was my turn to become agitated. It was as if the Universe had thrown down the gauntlet and I had nowhere else to run. My shames and secrets made up my very own 'shack' and were here on the other side of the world with me. The book in question was 'The Shack' by Wm Paul Young. I realised that if I was going to be truly happy, I could not keep my secret from my husband. I had to have a relationship that held no secrets, no shame.

Courage would be needed. Thankfully the tooth extraction had given me a taste for it. My life would never be the same again. It took me six months to build the courage to fully reveal my secret to my husband and another six to have the courage to surrender completely to GOD. In doing so, I experienced that my own soul was more beautiful than I could have imagined, and my faith that I was loveable was returning. Now, nine years later there is not a week goes by that I don't thank GOD for sending that book to me via my beautiful husband. He has always surprised me, and continues to surprise me in his capacity to love, to forgive, to have faith in love, and to have faith in me. It is the best gift anyone could ever receive.

Whilst writing this book I listened to Oprah interview the author of 'The Shack' Wm Paul Young and heard for the first time his actual personal story. It was his own experience of surrendering to his shameful secret of adultery that had made the existence of the book possible. If there was ever a doubt in my mind that we are all connected, that we are all one, it evaporated on that journey. It is also why I knew I had to share my own shame and my surrender in order to help readers who are struggling with their own secrets and shame.

You are more courageous than you know. You are more loved than you can imagine, it's now time to set yourself free. I can't promise it's easy and it will lead to things seemingly falling apart, but like the phoenix, the transformation and the life awaiting you on the other side is really quite miraculous.

Question the thoughts that drain you

Have you ever noticed how a thought can leave you feeling drained. You focus on this thought over and over, moment after moment. Maybe while doing the laundry, cooking a meal, walking the dog, while someone is talking to you and the thought is there, turning over and over keeping you in a trance. Focusing on negative thoughts is like filling a gorgeous bubble bath – hopping in and then immediately pulling the plug, so that within minutes your source of warmth and vitality has been drained away – leaving you exposed and more than a bit dissatisfied. That would be a crazy way to take a bath and yet it is how we live our lives day in and day out, if we do not question the thoughts that drain us of our vital life force.

Following my inner guidance whilst researching and writing this book, I spent time watching a Netflix series called 'Once Upon a Time'. In 'Once Upon a Time' land, the characters are truly themselves, but the wicked queen has placed a curse on the land so no one remembers who they truly are. For the past 28 years they have been living in a different, less magical, reality. They live in a modern world which is a big foggy in the detail. They have thoughts which conflict with their feelings, and narratives of lives, which just don't feel right. They are in jobs, which feel strange and are without true loving relationships. No one is truly themselves – stuck between the illusion and the glorious reality.

The only way to break the spell and set themselves free from the thoughts draining them of their true essence is to start to question these thoughts. And to choose to act differently from the way the thoughts and the story narrative, governed by these thoughts, would have them act. This isn't easy, it's no walk in the park and just like our inner critic, the wicked queen is there, filling them with self-doubt. It takes tons of self-trust and persistence, but it pays off. This is where the magic happens – small changes emerge in their daily lives and in the lives of those around them, because they are finally waking up to the fact that the thoughts that don't feel good, need to be questioned and the truth will set them free.

It's time to get into the habit of questioning your thoughts, which don›t feel good and come back to your true reality.

I remember, vividly, standing in my bedroom in July 2010 when a realisation hit me – maybe I had some things wrong? I don't mean I'd done things wrong – I've done many things wrong and I'm sure like every other human being I received feedback almost instantly about these wrong-doings. No, I'm referring to the realisation that the thoughts I'd based my actions and behaviour on, were not necessarily true. I thought about my former boss, old school friends, family members and my husband. As I re-called various scenarios, I realised I had never once, paused to consider whether the thoughts in my head were true. Thoughts such as:

"He doesn't actually like me."

"They will be angry with me."

"They think I'm boring."

"They don't like me."

"He will never forgive me."

I just believed them and because I did, I showed up so differently. One of my favourite confidence boosting mantras I use to override old fears is by Byron Katie. It's great if you find yourself in fear and full of doubt, especially if you are about to enter a room full of people.

"Everyone in here loves me, they just don't know it yet".

Imagine how differently you might show up if this was the thought you entered with, instead of any of the above. Questioning our thoughts is a huge part of the secret to being happier, and it is something we either will, or will not, do everyday and it will make all the difference.

It is only by loving ourselves for all of who we are, both the light and the dark, will we then be able to love others in the same way. What illusionary thoughts are keeping you stuck in a trance-like-state like the characters from *Once Upon a Time*? Which thoughts leave you feeling drained and powerless or just a bit blah? We don't need to let our power source drain away unnecessarily. We don't have to buy into a reality, which doesn't feel good without questioning that reality. Take the thoughts out of your mind, stare them down, shake them out and ask them the question that has magical power – is this really true?

Our bodies know the answers – we recognise the truth in how we feel. We need to trust these bodily feelings far more than we currently do. So we are fully able to use our precious energy to create a magical life. Only then, when the story of our life is told, it too may start with the magical words Once Upon a time...

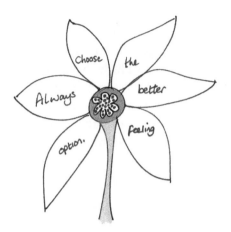

Always choose
the better
feeling option

In the five days, leading up to my time spent in the Priory I'd started to look back at my life and reflect. We had just returned from holiday on the Isle of Wight. Ironically, we had stayed at a hotel complex also called the Priory Bay. During our time there, we celebrated our daughters ninth birthday. On the morning of her birthday, I had slipped out very early down to the beautiful sandy beach. My plan was to write a birthday message in the sand for her, with the idea being, that she would discover it later that morning. After a few minutes gathering stones and shells, I became very still on the beach and just stared at my feet on the sand. It was as if a really important memory from my childhood was trying to break through to me – but try as I might I couldn't quite get there. Back in North Berwick, because of thoughts stirred-up by reading Wm Paul Young's 'Shack' I knew I needed to discover my own true thoughts. Deep down I knew I had felt very connected as a young child. And because of my soul searching, living by the sea and spending literally days at a time barefoot, an early childhood memory resurfaced. I think this is my earliest memory and is no doubt why I felt inspired to call my company Barefoot Ambition.

It's a really hot summer. I am three-years-old and sitting on my bottom on the warm concrete. The sun is beating down and squeals of laughter and shouts from my brothers, sisters and neighbouring children can be heard in the distance. My legs are wet from splashing at the outside tap. My chubby hands discover handfuls of sand spilling out from the newly laid lawn's edge, which I drop on to my legs. I do this again and again. I give my legs a little shake, my eyes light up and with a broad smile I exclaim; *"My legs are gold, my legs are gold! I'm magic, I can do magic".* I giggle and clamber up, admiring my self-created golden legs. Amongst the bustle of the other children, I make my way to the outside tap in the back garden to clean the sand off. I then head back to the front garden to, once again, make my magic. I do this all morning – totally content, totally self-satisfied.

This memory enabled me to ask myself some important questions:

"When did you get so angry?"

"When did you become so judgemental?"

"When did you stop feeling such deep joy?"

"When did you last smile, so wide, you could feel your face crack open?"

That day, as a small child, I simply chose what felt better for me. Every time we do that, we are connecting to the guidance of the Divine.

That warm glow inside is a divine combustion and is the powerful feedback from choosing the better-feeling option in any situation. You deserve to feel good in your life. You deserve to feel good about who you are, where you are from, your skin colour, the religion you were born with and whatever sexual preference you have. All of these are sacred and divine.

When ever you steer away from them and choose the option that feels worse, your body talks a different language. Your throat might constrict, you might have a tight chest – over time you might become increasingly anxious. You are denying your greatness and sacredness when you do not honour your true feelings.

If everyone on the planet chose what genuinely felt better for them – it would indeed, be heavenly for all. But we cannot wait for others to give us permission to do this. We must take responsibility to do this for ourselves. As Gandhi said; *"Be the change that you want to see in the world."*

Do what feels better and your world will change. Everyone wins when you chose the better-feeling option and some people really need to hear you say 'no'. People need to feel what is true for them, when you speak truly to them. We attract people, who are playing their part, to try and help us be true to ourselves. Everyone is craving authentic, everyone wants to feel better – the simple truth is, we are only ever one decision away from giving ourselves what we have been searching for.

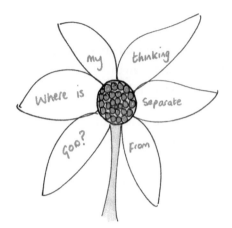

Where is my thinking separate from God?

As I write a nightly journal, one of the things I notice, is that some days I feel so blessed, so loved, so in tune with the Divine that my gratitudes flow easily from my pen but other nights – well not so much. I pause and have to dig deeper. These are often the days where I have been lost in my head and judged myself over and over, without even realising it. When I pause, I am aware my thinking has been separate from GOD that day. I have not seen the things she sees and my idea of me, and this world is very different from hers.

To me GOD means literally everything and I believe we are all made from that divine spark. It's the air we breathe and the wind in our sails. It's the peace in our hearts, but it's the rage too. It's the imperfections, it's the mistakes, it's getting it wrong, GOD is with us through it all.

So much of how we live our lives by, has be made up – man-made guidelines, man-made rules and man-made judgements. If any of these rules, guidelines and judgements cause another harm, or deem another as inferior then this is an example of when our think-ing is off-base from GOD.

There is a wonderful book, I would highly recommend, by Neale Donald Walsch called *"God's Message to the World: You've Got Me All*

Wrong". Do you really believe the old story? When you look at the stars at night, don't the rules, the guidelines, and the judgements in religious doctrine seem a tad inaccurate? God does not need our love, our obedience, our sacrifice, no more than the sun needs us to say good morning to it so it can come out and shine.

The GOD I experienced, which I feel, guiding me daily, is an energy, which is loving, and beautifully welcoming. And, just like the sun, it is always there, needing no thanks or praise. Nothing I had been taught before, matched the GOD I experienced in the Priory. In that moment I realised my pre-conditioned thinking had been so separate from GOD's.

Let's see how this misunderstanding might play out in our daily lives:

We don't tell our partner we have made a mistake because we think they will leave us and hate us – and yet our silence separates us anyway. Our thinking is separate from GOD.

We don't say no to a request which drains us again and again, because we think it would make us a selfish person or we have no choice. Our thinking is separate from GOD.

We look in the mirror and judge who we see and wish ourselves away. Our thinking is separate from GOD.

We don't ask for help when we really need it because we think others will think we are weak. Our thinking is separate from GOD.

But,

When we honour our feelings and we speak our truth – in that moment, GOD is speaking.

When we say no to someone else because it doesn't feel good – we are saying yes to the GOD inside.

When we ask for help by willing to be vulnerable – in that moment we are GODly.

When we look into the mirror and smile at who we see – in that moment we are looking into the eyes of the one and only GOD.

GOD – Glorious Onward Direction.

My love for you is eternal

I remember looking at this doodle before I went to a cross-fit session one Friday morning. Moments later, standing in front of the bathroom mirror, looking into my eyes, I decided to repeat the words; "my love for you is eternal". I felt a strong emotion rising and I said it again; "my love for you is eternal", adding; "all of you, all of who you are – I will never abandon you". Again, I could feel my emotions rise.

The cross-fit session was particularly tough me for. The inexplicable feeling of being close to tears was strong, and I wondered which part or parts of me I had awoken with my words to myself in the mirror earlier that morning. I began to think of the little girl who had felt crushed and confused when her teachers praised her art, but her classmates disliked that her art was being praised. And I heard myself whisper; "it's okay, we are okay, my love for you is eternal". I managed to finish my workout but shared, with the group, I was feeling really teary and was rewarded with a spontaneous group hug, which felt wonderful. I felt my little-self right there with us, letting her know we are allowed to express our emotions and there is an abundance of love around us always, the words in the flower-doodle echoing over and over.

Later that day, a dear friend was looking at a photo taken of my husband and me – a couple of years before my time in the Priory. It's a lovely picture, lots of people comment on it, we look so happy. We had been skiing on our own for a few days and this photo was taken by one of the roving photographers. But looking at it always caused bittersweet, memories. My friend and I chatted about my thoughts then, and how the thoughts and secret shames I carried with me, which popped to mind, as the photo was taken, had always tainted my view of that image. It felt as if I was a fraud, as if I was a fake – but really I had been a victim of my own thoughts.

Many beautiful, magical times can be ruined by our unquestioned thoughts, telling us lies – taking away from our natural joy. This is why it is crucial we realise, we are not our thoughts, and the thoughts causing suffering need to be questioned. My friend had always loved the photo of my husband and me but she now understood why I always looked wistful when she'd previously admired it. So there and then, I looked at the figures in the photo with new eyes and to both my husband and myself, I whispered once more; *"my love for you is eternal"*. The women in the photo needed to feel that too.

The lie of *'I am not enough'* needs to end here for all of us. Each and every human being is fed the lie and the reality is GOD's love for us is eternal. You feel it fully when you own the Divine, residing deep inside you, beginning the journey to love all parts of you – past and present.

Take a moment to look in the mirror today and say the words I did. Pay attention to any emotions and memories that arise. A version of you that needs loving attention should make him or herself known. Take the chance to send this message loud and clear and in the process you are bringing another part of yourself home.

19

Your story hides
the real you

It had been an unusual day in my home town of North Berwick when I chose this card. Snow had descended, closing schools and businesses, delivery trucks could not get in to town and with this interruption the realities of daily life disappeared under this a blanket of snow.

As an intuitive coach I guide people, helping them question their current story so they can create a new, more empowering one. I help them step outside a limiting story. I help them question the story of their 'conditioning' so the actual truth of who they truly are can be revealed. Most people who come to me are ready to do this – they have usually experienced something a bit like a snowstorm, where suddenly nothing looks the same, their internal landscape has changed and they have the new-found ability to step outside their own story. This presents a blank canvas with which they can make new footsteps.

In the beginning of this new story, things can feel very serene, calm and everything looks beautiful. But as with snow, as the temperature rises the snow melts, and the serene landscape often reveals even more mud than before. Like I did, my clients often struggle with losing their new-found serenity and judge themselves harshly.

But nothing has gone wrong because, it is through our stories, we find the hidden parts of ourselves. These stories are essential for healing but we can only do this because we are no longer in 'the story'. We are simply looking at it. In this place we are no longer hiding – we are simply seeking the parts of us that are.

I often tell clients that we are on a treasure hunt to find the parts of themselves that are not up to speed with the truth of their brilliance, the parts that are 'stuck'. The parts in hiding oblivious to the fact that things worked out really well. That it is okay to be heard now and they are totally loved. These parts are yet to awaken as they are hiding in our sub-conscious. Together we can find the parts, which are playful, trusting and honest – we even bring back the loud and supposedly crazy parts. I help them bring back the dreamer and the adventurer. We bring back the parts, which are willing to feel more, the parts, which trust their intuition and the parts, which are far from self-conscious. In every treasure hunt the reunions are always incredible.

But something is essential for this, something we underestimate, and that is, understanding there is life after the perfect storm. The daily interactions, the slushy parts, the stuff which makes us slip and stumble because they activate the feelings which will help us locate the hidden parts of ourselves – the parts that are now ready to be found. These daily moments, after the momentary stillness, are the essential clues that we need to go on this this treasure hunt, and in the process we will write a new, expanded eternal story.

20

It's okay not to know and need help

One of the issues, which get in our way, is the never-ending voice in our head – the human inner critic. As a woman I refer to this critic in the female form but men may wish to refer to it as a male voice. She is the voice telling us to do something, then criticises us, for doing it. Of course she has a purpose, and I would like to make it clear that the inner critic is part of our shadow-side, and needs our love and guidance too. On many occasions she is trying to keep us safe and will have guided us to safety in the past. Yet she doesn't expand with us, so is rarely up to speed about what we are actually capable of, and she has always needed guidance. We just forgot that it is us who has to guide her. I think of her as the over-stressed PA whose boss has gone away, ignoring her responsibility of being the CEO of her own life. The PA is doing the best she can, but it's not her job to be the CEO so she firefights and sees many things as being a threat to her absent boss.

After the Priory, even with my new sense of self, I would continue to be plagued with self-doubt. This was frustrating because I knew deep down these thoughts were not true, but I didn't understand what was going on, and I couldn't seem to hear the truth. At school, it would seem I had not paid attention in biology, because I'm unsure if we covered the fight or flight response. I definitely do not remember being taught about the amygdala. I find the explanation of the amygdala incredible, and I was fascinated to be told that our fear responses are generally outdated. In fact, they are prehistoric. Let me describe a scenario that could explain why we behave the way we do.

Imagine you are four-years-old and at school for the first time. It's break-time and you're given a bottle of milk and a straw. The bottle has a foil topping on it. You know its milk, as it looks vaguely familiar, you have big bottles of this at home. But you've never been given a straw and a bottle of your own before – your mother takes care of that. Everything is always shared out and as the fourth child of the family you always watch what your siblings do first. So, you watch and try to copy someone who seems to know what to do. The straw goes in – all good – but on autopilot you tip the bottle up to drink through this new straw-thing and suddenly you are covered in milk. There are sniggers and you freeze and puff, the memory fades. But in that moment you can imagine feeling foolish, and there she is, your inner critic; "*Look what you did stupid-pants*"

In that moment new – but not so bright and shiny – neural pathways are formed. We always forge two at the same time.

"*When I try something new I get it wrong, I am stupid, I am not as capable as other kids, this feels horrible.*" And another rant from the inner critic; "*why didn't you wait, you went too fast, they laughed at us*".

Maybe, like me, every time you attempt something new, that same negative feeling is re-triggered, and you learn to pause, to copy, to follow – reluctant to try new things, afraid to make mistakes – all in a tiny unsettled human moment.

Yes, the girl was me. Why is it one of my strongest memories of my first experience of school? Because it is these memories that set the thermostat for how we behave going forward – so much of my school experience was tempered by that one moment. But, I now see all of my life events have been created by my own thoughts, and it was always in my hands to behave or act differently. Because I remembered this, I could start to break the pattern.

What do I finally recognise is okay to do?

I now ask for help – something I found almost impossible to do. Now when I'm unsure about something, instead of trying to figure it out or get in a stew about it – I pause, smile, remind myself and my inner critic; *"If you don't know, you don't know, that's totally okay, ask someone. You are not meant to know, if you don't know."*

I've replayed the milk moment over and over again, both in my childhood and adult life. I believed I should know things I didn't, and I would bluff my way through instead of confessing I was unsure. Unknowingly, I limited myself from emotionally maturing. The inner critic is not to be underestimated, and we really need to shine the light of awareness on her presence – too many of us are still in the dark about her existence.

In 2010, whilst undertaking a Life Coaching Certification, I took part in an online webinar course with coaches from America. I needed to find other coaches who were talking about their inner wisdom, as I knew tapping into mine was my number one priority if I was to become an energy coach. I value tools hugely, but none more so, than drawn out information and guidance from inside ourselves, and this course was perfect for that. The three coaches – Martha Beck, Dr Lissa Rankin and Amy Aylers – spoke with such passion about overcoming the inner critic and tapping into inner wisdom, I was hooked!

The 1:1 with the inner critic.

I sometimes call my inner critic 'Martha', and although she can be mean I do not hate her – quite the opposite. I now acknowledge her, reassure her, and often find myself shaking my head and laughing with her. Our inner critic, our ego-part, is still part of who, we have to love and cherish.

However, I am totally committed to keeping her in check, even though I find myself laughing at her naughtiness as one would when listening to a toddler or dealing with a naughty spaniel – something I seem to do a lot of, these days! The inner critic needs to be guided and given jobs to do that serve us better. My inner critic or PA is great at remembering names so I rely on her to whisper them to me at times.

Amy Aylers, during the coaching, described a process she uses – a quick three-step process – and over the last few years I have shared my own version of that process with clients, most of the time with stunning effects. This process, in different forms, has been echoed by many other coaches I admire and respect, and it taps right into the experience I had in 2010.

When I experienced, what I call, 'my big awakening' a strong confident voice inside me, spoke very clearly and I followed her instruction fully. But in the year following, I was unable to hear her voice as clearly, and I found this frustrating. Then along came these three coaches (thank you Universe!) and I was able to practice silencing my inner critic so my inner wisdom could be heard more clearly. If you like journaling then this technique will be very powerful for you.

For over five years I have been using this process myself, and with clients either on a one-to-one basis or in my workshops all dealing with the same issue – being too hard on ourselves. We have to own our light, thereby shining a light on the dark psyche rogue in our brain, so the light of our inner divine wisdom can burst through and guide us onwards.

Exercise

Step one:

If you are feeling negative and your head is whispering thoughts that do not serve you well that is your inner critic talking. You are not and I repeat you are NOT your thoughts! To take charge of this rogue critic and the mean inner dialogue, which, if left unchecked, will lead you spiralling into more self-doubt and negativity – speak to your inner critic and say the following;

"*Okay* (naming her is optional – but fun) *give me your all.*"

Have a pen and paper handy and just let your inner critic vent, yes, the whole shebang. Do not censor yourself. No one in the world will ever read this, not even you will read again as you will be destroying it immediately afterwards. These toxic words, which are there and keeping you feeling 'bla' will no longer be stuck, festering inside you. You will be a bit shocked at what comes out, and you may get upset – that's normal and it's totally okay. Better out than in, has never been truer!

Step two:

Thank your inner critic and acknowledge her perspective. Then rip or burn what you have written – just let it go. Take a deep breath and if necessary have a sip of water. Then get another sheet of paper, change your pen colour too, if possible, take another deep breath – and invite your inner wisdom to speak;

"Inner wisdom could you please give me your perspective on this please?"

This permission to speak is really important as it gives your wonderful inner wisdom, your Divine eternal self the space to come forward. Your inner wisdom is never pushy! So, you have taken a deep breath, invited your inner wisdom to speak, now write down, in a letter format, whatever comes out. Start with; *Dear (your name)*. You will know it's your inner wisdom by the change of tone and although you may not want to hear what she or he is saying, she will say it with such warmth and compassion it will feel like love. Sign off; *Love from your inner wisdom*. Remember what your favourite teacher sounded like? Good you are on track!

Step three:

Repeat your inner wisdom's words to yourself in the mirror, if there is one. Anchor the memory and feeling of them, somewhere in your being, by either holding your hand over your heart or tapping your wrist. This is a Neural Linguistic Pathway technique and it really helps to absorb the message.

Step four:

Take action – trust the message, absorb it – do as you are instructed. Keep your inner wisdom's letter and return to the message when necessary, or repeat this exercise where necessary over any other troubling thought.

And there you have it – a simple yet incredibly powerful tool, which enables you to learn to trust yourself more. It will release anger and frustration without causing harm to anyone else. It can help you overcome anxiety, become braver and follow your own intuition more.

Making mistakes is an essential part of being human

I've written about the embarrassment and paralysis I felt as a young school child when I got things wrong. Of course, now I see making mistakes is part of the human experience and are essential. However, as a child any time I got something wrong, my default was to either feel embarrassed, ashamed or to blame someone else. Ever heard the words; *"Now look at what you made me do"* – that is a line deep in my subconscious. One of my primary school teachers had an interesting approach to mistakes, two strikes on the hands with a metre ruler was her favourite. No doubt that was where the embarrassment factor came from.

As a parent, I wish I could say I was the type of mum who had an enlightened approach to my children's mistakes when they were small. But because of my own perspective this simply wasn't always true. My children were seven and nine when things changed massively for me. I'm sure all parents make mistakes and that is partly our job, we learn from them and try to get things better the next time. However, the more loving we are to ourselves the more we can be truly present with our children and show up fully which ensures we understand that mistakes are essential.

American author and motivational speaker Jack Canfield shares a story, in one of his books, he'd heard in a radio interview. The story really touched me and affirmed two things. Firstly, making mistakes is essential for success and it really can make a difference, if you are taught from a young age that it's okay and safe to make them. Secondly, that being self-loving leads to being a more present parent. A famous researcher attributed his successful career to knowing it was okay to make mistakes from an early age. At the age of two, feeling thirsty and using his own initiative, he tried to take a large bottle of milk from the fridge. He lost his grip and spilt the milk all over the kitchen floor. His mother didn't scold him but actually praised the mess. She let him play in the spilt milk before they cleared it up, together. Referring to the experience as a failed experiment in how to carry a large bottle of milk with two tiny hands! Plus, he was learning how to clean up after his mistakes too. They then went outside, to the garden, and she let him practice carrying the bottle again and again. That morning, he claims, he learnt it was safe to make mistakes and there is always an opportunity to learn from them. I can't think of a better start for a man of research.

Perhaps, in our own lives we have not had such a positive early learning experience so the fear of making mistakes keeps us stuck. It certainly never leads to progress. It denies us the opportunity to feel our way through things and to grow from our very valid experiences. Yet, making mistakes is an essential part of being human and it means we are unable to fully embrace our humanity if we do not accept that mistakes are inevitable. As a consequence people often get put on pedestals – until they get it wrong, which they will – and others get polarised, all because of a ridiculous notion that we are not meant to get any of this human experience wrong. As spiritual teacher Eckhart Tolle so beautifully says in his book the 'The Power of Now' – we become victims of victims, as the fear of making mistakes permeates through our subconscious from one generation to another.

Why do I believe we are meant to get it wrong? Because I believe we came here to have the whole experience – the good, the bad and the ugly. And in the midst of making all our mistakes we'll finally remember we are 'the Divine loving presence' and that there is no external God judging us from on high. Once we acknowledge this, we get to experience being that loving presence.

During my stint as a radio presenter I made the classic radio-presenter mistake – I left the microphone on as we went to an ad-break. My guest and I chatted away, with the belief no one else was listening, and just as I realised my error and turned the microphone off, I received a couple of texts revealing that others, were indeed, able to hear us loud and clear. This mistake provided me with the opportunity to own *'I'm only human on-air and if I am going to do things I'm going to make mistakes as I do them. It's part of being human.'* No one actually trusts total perfection. It also gave me the opportunity to practice self-compassion stopping my inner critic in her tracks. It made me see that the young girl terrified of getting things wrong in primary school was no longer in the driving seat. Finally it made us laugh and, if anything else, it helps me remember that most of our mistakes are never worth getting our knickers in a twist over!

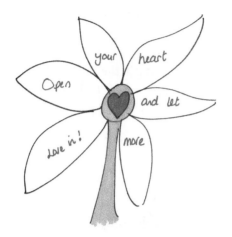

Open your heart and let more love in

All too often we may unknowingly have closed our hearts. Maybe we were once hurt badly so our brain sends us a message – don't do that again it's too scary, it hurts too much, we can't handle it.

But our heart cannot actually, be broken – it has the capacity to feel so much, it's the reason we came here, to experience the good, the bad, the ugly. It has the capacity for much more love than our minds would have us believe.

Getting hurt and feeling rejection is part of life. Yes, it's not great when it hurts, but it does not matter how bruised or broken your heart may feel at times, shutting it down, is not the solution. That means fear is winning and the most important lesson I have learnt on my journey, so far, is that fear must not be allowed to make any of our ongoing decisions. We have to be willing to feel everything if we truly want to live our lives as a full expression of who we are.

I remember a day, when I was about five-years-old, having a wonderful time playing with chalk and a duster at the class black-board. Lost in a creative moment, using the duster to carve out the shape and the features, I created a picture of a large chicken. As I stepped back to look at my creation my teacher became aware of what I was doing. She thought it was wonderful and gave me a lot of praise. She suddenly rushed next door and moments later returned with another teacher to show my work off. However, as they returned another child started to rub out my picture. The teacher became very cross and told her off quite harshly. Resulting in the child giving me the nastiest glare in return, as if it were my fault – I felt terrible. In the same moment I experienced praise I also felt real pain.

We need to use our hearts in everything – these early memories from as young as five-years-old reveal to me that I experienced praise and pain simultaneously. And because of a dark belief self-planted in my mind at the age of three, that I wasn't loveable, I was getting good at putting barriers up. The following quotes help us understand how important it is to forge new ways of living with an open heart in all areas.

> *"Love is what we are born with fear is what we learn here"* – Marianne Williamson

> *"Love is our true power"* – Robert Holden

I was prematurely self-critical and self-conscious, particularly in relation to my early passions of art, dancing and singing. It felt too scary to allow myself open-hearted expression in these areas, because in the moment of praise from teachers came sneers from others. I found myself, at a very young age, believing praise would also cause people to resent me. So, I put barriers around my heart, with regards to doing things I loved, as it hurt too much. What I didn't understand then, is as I have mentioned in previous scenarios that the neural pathways in our brain are forged in pairs and, in my case, praise accompanied pain. This is why we associate one thing with another – chocolate and joy, for example. Early childhood experiences forge neural pathways, which pop up together, again and again, and they can either be inspiring or limiting.

Thankfully I now recognise a limiting pathway and have learnt to sidestep the auto-response, no longer letting fear of rejection or jealously stop me creating the things, which cause myself and others joy.

In which area of your life do you need to open your heart more, to let more love in? What is it you would really love to do? It's time to take a leap of faith, as love really is your true power. So, if you feel drawn to investigate something, to explore a new experience, trust me when I say – that's all the permission you actually need.

Keeping yourself small serves absolutely no one

"I am such an idiot..." were the words, a really lovely, secure-sounding woman said at the end of an interview with a radio presenter. I was driving, listening to her telling her very funny story – which according to the presenter had made her day. This woman, by sharing her story, had contributed joy to many. So when she signed off by saying; *"I am such an idiot"* I wanted to reach into the radio and take her face in my hands and say; *"Don't ever say that, no you are not!"*

In that same moment I remembered the countless times I had finished a story by criticising myself in the same way. It feels as if those words sum up the human conundrum. I do not speak to myself like this anymore – it's a major no-no and I know it makes a massive difference.

We think we are idiots – when we are not, we think we are stupid – when we are not, we think we are rubbish – when that is far from the truth. Think about how often you say a, seemingly, harmless derogatory comment to yourself or in the company of others. And whilst we shrug our shoulders and say, it's only a saying, we don't necessarily believe this. In fact, we are reinforcing our subconscious mind to believe the things we say – with the dangerous auto response of 'everything is our fault.'

The woman, on the radio, was sharing a funny story about how her child's nursery teacher found a pair of her knickers in her son's school bag. When asked, by the presenter, how they came to be there – she genuinely had no idea. Laughing with the presenter, she attributed it to some freak laundry accident! At the end of the story she called herself an idiot – illustrating how often we find fault with ourselves and take blame for things that cannot be explained. Who knows? Her child may have put them there, or anyone else in the house, perhaps the cat or even the dog! Yet she calls herself the idiot.

How does this manifest in an unhealthy way? As humans we think when things go wrong, someone is at fault, someone is an idiot – and we usually always blame ourselves, we shame ourselves over and over again. Our subconscious mind is tuned into this, so when something bigger does actually happen through no fault of our own, we still blame ourselves.

When I was 14, walking home from school one day, a man exposed himself to me. Sure enough, in my mind, I felt I was to blame. For days, years even, I told myself I was an idiot. I am sure that in the moment this incident occurred, my subconscious was so full of; "*I am such an idiot*", that my reaction was to freeze. No doubt it was due to the fact, that as children, we constantly witness grown-ups berate themselves for even the smallest of errors. This kind of mental self-bullying shuts us down and prevents us from getting the support we need, when we need it. Maybe we are convinced this is what people think of us, so we speak negatively to ourselves, hoping it will hurt less – but the truth is, no one can hurt us, like we hurt ourselves. We bully ourselves; we undermine our beautiful hearts day-in and day-out with derogatory comments. But, as grown ups, we need to remember that children hear and are influenced greatly by what we say. It's time to pay more attention to our verbal commentary and, just take a breath, rather than attack. Our subconscious mind needs us to feed new words to it, so that in times of real difficulty it will help us, not paralyse us. I have long since healed my 14 year-old self and her beautiful, friendly heart is free to be once more.

Think about the words you use to describe yourself and instead of the usual suspects, next time you look in the mirror, try these;

"*I am amazing*"

"*I am funny*"

"*I am the queen/king in my own parade*"

"*I am the one and only me*"

"*I am doing the best I can*"

"*I am a miracle of matter*"

"*I am blessed to be me*"

"*I am dancing to my own tune*"

"*I am still here*"

"*I am showing up*"

"*I am stronger than you know*"

And, if you are finishing an awesome story, like the woman on the radio, before you end with a derogatory comment please – just stop, smile and breathe. And be happy that people are more than likely thinking; "*you are a carrier of joy*".

Breathe deeply
and return
back home

As an energy coach, I am, fascinated by the subject of energy. After the Priory it became impossible not to see a rise and fall in my own energy levels, and I invested time and money in really getting to grips with my own vibrational levels.

A couple of years ago I succumbed to a new addiction, in the form of watching 'The Vampire Diaries' on Netflix. My gorgeous teenage daughter lures me into watching these gems of wisdom, but not before my inner critic has a go at my supposed laziness. My inner critic is eventually quietened as my enjoyment kicks in and the great, and often inspirational, lines grab my attention. It helps that the vampires in the series are gorgeous – but actually, these gorgeous creatures gave me an insight into the whole concept of energy vampires.

Energy vampires are considered to be people who energetically bleed you dry – those people who, after spending time with, make you feel awful. There is a school of thought even in the healing and spiritual world that doesn't own the part we play in attracting these energy vampires. However, I believe, we are all capable of being an energy vampire – there is one inside all of us. Indeed, this validates us having to accept the light and the dark parts of us all.

If the thought; *"some people just suck the life out of me"* resonates with you – consider this. I believe this is something you consented to, based upon, your current perspective and vibrational level. Do not continue with the belief that you need to hide from vampires and wear a metaphorical protective cross to stop them draining you. Instead take control of the power source inside of you and change your perception.

In *'The Vampire Diaries'*, as in all classic vampire stories, vampires can only enter homes with an invitation. In this story there is a baddy called Vampire Klaus. He is a nasty piece of work, having wreaked havoc for one thousand years. Full of self-loathing and with little understanding of love, he has no real friends and has shut his family out. But even with his dark powers he could not enter into a home without permission. Vampires, literally, cannot cross the threshold of a home without the owner's permission. They cannot get close to harm you, or suck the life force out of you and this is the same with energy vampires. You have to invite them in; you have to give them permission to enter. You have the power to say yes or no.

But what happens when the characters are not in their homes? It seemed, in the story, only certain people attracted vampires into their lives in the first place, whilst others remained oblivious. And there were some characters, who were more than happy to be around vampires yet were never drained. Perhaps the answer is in the expression 'home is where the heart is'.

When you are fully in the moment, when you accept all of who you are, when you like then love who you are, when you feel content in your own skin – you, literally, are at home in your own skin. When this happens you gain present body awareness at home with your beating heart. So, your intuition will guide you and you won't find yourself in a place where you might be attacked by needy, reckless vampires. Being in love with who you are, feeling at home in all parts of you, is a clear 'energetic' signal to any supposed energy vampires that they cannot take from you. Energetically you create a protective shield, you are totally at home, and Source is all around you.

However, if you are lost in thought, perpetually fretting about the future, full of regret about the past or worried about being loved and liked, and find it hard to say no – you will not be fully present in your body. So energetically you are saying, 'come on in, bleed me dry'. Ignoring your inner guidance telling you when and where you could be and who you could spend time with to ensure an energetically joyous experience, means you give the green light to all those around you who are in need of energy from you. Because, of course, they themselves are not happy in their skin and believe they have to be nourished and fed from an external source – their inner vampire will bleed you dry.

There is a flip side to this. Perhaps you might be feeling lousy and you bump into, or spend time with someone who feels like a willing energy donor – you will leave them feeling so much better, but crucially, they don't feel drained as a result. A misunderstanding and judgement about energy alignment can occur where you are feeling miserable and don't expect joyous people to come into your reality. However, in this situation your honest feelings have been felt, by the Universe and, at the same time, the energy donors have given the Universe the signal to allow others in need of love and energy, to come into their reality. It is effortless for them to be in your company and not feel drained, because in that moment they love who they are and are not in a place of fear – your inner vampire is fed, without attacking, because of the higher vibration of love.

We are all made of energy, and our energy levels, our vibrations are changeable. With this awareness we have the ability to stabilise our vibration, control it, and keep raising it. We are not in need of others' approval, attention or love to the degree that we will deny who, we are because we now believe we are able to create this for ourselves. We love and approve of ourselves. We love and cherish the skin that we are in. This is simply mirrored back to us, by those we allow in, and it feels good, but most importantly it has been created by us – by how we feel inside.

The experience of feeling sucked dry or depleted, is merely a feedback mechanism that shows you need to focus on loving and nurturing your own needs more than you are. Doing things and being with people, who mirror how you are currently feeling simply shows your current vibrational level. If this doesn't feel good, then the time has come once again to take your power back, and start saying a few more no's. "*No*", can be said with love and a smile too. But remember it's also a full sentence. Here are a few to practice and remember it's the energy it matches, which is important; "*NO*." "*I love you, but, NO.*" "*Thanks so much, but I'm a NO.*"

So, yes, energy vampires exist – but they do so in all of us. We move away from being an energy vampire into the frequency of a willing energy donor, when we love and cherish who we are. And when we don't allow other active energy vampires to drain us, it starts to feel effortless. We do this by listening to our body signals so our internal inner wisdom can guide us. This can only happen when we are fully present in our bodies. This means coming back to our breath – stopping, pausing, especially before committing and agreeing to something.

We will, of course, even with this awareness, experience what feels like an attack or experience someone not wanting to be around us. But this is valuable feedback, plus it is really a great opportunity to return into our bodies, to connect with our heart, our home. It's also a chance to find what our heart desires and give ourselves a well needed break, knowing the sun will rise on another new day – one where vampires will not come our way!

25

The sweetness lies in total surrender

Growing up in Northern Ireland the word surrender was associated with giving up, losing. I was brought up as a Catholic in a largely Protestant community and although the word 'surrender' is often associated with a loyalist stance – all people in Northern Ireland, regardless of their religious or political stance, absorbed its meaning in the same way.

I am often asked; how I became more at peace with who I am and how did I learn to love myself in a compassionate way. If I trace the essential steps in that process – surrender is one of them. I really do mean it when I say; "*the sweetness lies in total surrender.*"

First comes acceptance – acceptance of who you are and whatever the situation you find yourself in. Next comes trust – a decision to trust the surrender is the only step possible for you to take.

So – acceptance, trust and surrender – three magical steps to your liberation.

We can apply these steps to every situation, again and again, and in my experience they come in this order. Yet, many of us have been programmed differently, it feels counter-intuitive to take these three steps – it feels alien.

Animals have a very different view of life and death to us. If you watch an animal of prey being hunted in a nature programme you may have noticed that at the moment of death the animal has totally surrendered. Its first reaction is to take flight or fight but if this is not successful, it will show a level of acceptance and totally surrender to its hunter. They know, when the game is up, they relax and let go. In this way they are not afraid of the transition that death provides.

As humans we are hard-wired to fight death to the bitter end, as particularly in the Western culture, we are taught death is final, our life has a final destination. Although there are many stories about humans finally surrendering to inevitable death and feeling at peace when they do – they are getting a glimpse, in that moment of surrender, that there is in fact more. Because of my experience in 2010, I believe the death of the human body does not signify the end of our life force but we will go onto another creative experience. What if we are eternal? Perhaps animals have always known and trusted this, which is why they surrender to death so easily.

But as beings with a consciousness, perhaps we don't necessarily have to die physically in this lifetime, to experience a new perspective, to experience a new life. We can let go of our old thoughts, beliefs and fears, and surrender to the Source – trusting that a new way of living a new life is possible.

Surrendering isn't something you can do verbally. You cannot simply say the words 'I surrender' and experience a new way of being. The power of surrender lies when we have no alternative, because, it's triggered by a deep acceptance, which in turn is triggered by a decision to finally trust that you cannot do this alone. In that moment you are surrendering to the light that you are – and you are letting go of the controls.

It's time to embrace a new alternative to the fight or flight paradigm – it's when we surrender that we become the light.

26

You always get to choose what you hear

Just like the word surrender means different things to different people, I've come to understand that even, within the same language, different words mean different things to us. Because we all have different meanings to similar words and in any conversation we are all listening through our own particular filter. What we hear will often depend on what narrative is running through our head at that time. Plus, what we hear is also a pretty good reflection, of how we speak to others. As we are often unaware of this, we may miss the tone we are sending out – it's via the response we become enlightened. As a mum of two teenagers it's all too easy for me to pick up on 'their tone' and not take any responsibility from where that comes. I have to take a step back and listen to myself.

As with anything relating to the complexities of being human there are layers and layers to this. Have you noticed when you are in a calm, peaceful mood you may respond differently to the same words that cause an angry reaction when you are not in that calm, peaceful place. Words such as defence, offence and striker don't just apply to the game of football – our conversations are littered with such behaviours. But, once we become aware of it, we can choose not only what we hear, but also what we say with more compassion. The tone and energy behind words can reveal a lot and if you choose to pay attention you will be able to hear the emotional need behind them.

When we understand we can choose what we hear – we don't have to take things literally, suddenly messages can sound very different. Behind words of attack are often feelings of jealousy, fear, pain and confusion. And, it is totally within our control whether we accept words of love and praise. Text messages are a great way of practising this – you can choose what tone you hear and this will lead to better conversations.

So as we navigate onwards, remember we all have filters, we all have our prejudices and our beliefs, which are unique to us, as do those we are listening to. Remember the words of Andrea Gardner; *"Beliefs give rise to thoughts and words which birth our actions"*. Sometimes we may have to accept home truths, and express deep gratitude. Other times we may choose to be motivated and inspired not give up in the face of naysayers. On another occasion we might realise someone is deeply hurting and needs our compassion. Ultimately we get to choose, and this is what will make the difference.

27

Everything is perfect for your growth

I'm going to share my reaction to the news, in 2016, that Donald Trump was to become the American President. This was the gift the news gave me;

"We are spiritual beings on a human journey, we are powerful beyond measure. It is only our mind that feed us lies that make us feel any differently."

As the results of the American elections were being announced, I was watching the news on television – deep down, my inner wisdom knew what was about to happen – but I was in denial. I hear the unmistakable announcement, that Donald Trump was the winning candidate. In front of my children I burst into tears. It was as if my bubble had burst and in that moment I heard my inner child say; *"How could that happen? How? It's impossible."*

I watched, transfixed and felt a huge wave of sadness, a grief but I also listened as I watched. Looking at Donald Trump, I chose not to hate and I focused on what I could love – and I loved his son. I saw a little boy, the same age as my son, weary to his bones, brave in his mission. How brave is he, to be Donald Trump's son, and I just felt pure love. Once the children headed off to school, I allowed my inner child to feel the sadness, the disbelief and discovered there was also, rising anger. In allowing myself to feel whatever I need to feel as part of my healing journey process, I remembered an incident from my childhood.

It's the late 70s, and I'm walking home from school with one of my brothers. I, literally, stop in my tracks when I hear him say; *"By the way have you heard the news? Santa has been killed in a helicopter crash."* I thought; *"How could that happen? How? It's impossible. But if it's true, it is so sad. I mean how could he die? What kind of world am I living in where Santa with all his superpowers dies in a helicopter crash?"*

In hindsight, I think my brother thought it would be kinder to tell me Santa had died, rather than the truth – he is not real. As perhaps he'd been told the year before. I don't remember the rest of the conversation and I know I didn't burst into tears – because in my view, at the age of nine, that would have been babyish and weak – remember my three-year-old self.

I did, what we humans do best, I buried my sadness and with it my belief in superpowers. I now realise a part of me stayed on that street, sad and angry for years – I so desperately wanted Santa to be real, because without that magic, this world felt horrible and I wanted the magical mystery, not reality.

Flash forward to Wednesday 9th November 2016. I hear the words that would, once again, burst my bubble. For a moment, I was tempted to cover my eyes to deny the darkness that felt real and present. I didn't want this reality, I didn't want to believe that hate had won, that we were going backwards, and that humanity is doomed because darkness is winning. But, instead of shutting down I became very present and, this time, my inner child felt safe to cry, and as she did I held her closely and allowed her to feel the grief, the sadness and the anger that she felt unable to, all those years ago. I took care of the part that was sad and angry, and I encouraged her to come back with me into the light of present time. There I showed her we can work with any reality, we are the magical, the mystical, our own superpower, and all the while I kept letting her feel whatever she needed to feel. I remembered I get to choose what affects my vibration, so I chose to lean on the part of me that whispered; *"Sweetheart I hold the power"*.

I had a shower, I put on cosy clothes and I walked along the high street to attend my Wednesday morning ritual of yoga. I acknowledged every person I came into eye contact with, sending love with every step and nod. I just let my feet walk and I trusted my body knew something my mind didn't. By the time I reached my destination, my inner child was still subdued but she now felt seen and safe at home. On meeting my yoga teacher Roxanna, she gave me the biggest hug and looked deeply into my eyes without one bit of fear. We shared our emotions, with one another. Roxanna felt something my inner child didn't so I allowed my inner child to feel that emotion and stay even more present, to resist the drama and to become very still. I let my inner child feel the reassurance that I had denied her all those years ago by burying it, thinking I was being strong because I didn't want to appear babyish.

There were over 15 people at yoga, that morning, no doubt, all feeling different things. The focus was on peace and by the end of the class, as I tuned into the birds singing outside, I felt deeply deeply at peace – I had begun to take my power back.

I know I needed to reclaim all the parts of me, stuck in time, which are full of fear or hatred, so I feel very strong and free. Then I can use my superpower, from within, for the good and be who I am meant to be – a light that doesn't run from the dark. If you feel anger that's okay, but allow that anger to ignite something deep inside you. Ignite the part, which knows Santa didn't hold the power and neither does Donald Trump, or any nation we deem to call a superpower. Nor does hate or fear.

But what if, this is the big wake up call? What if Donald Trump is actually our most essential spiritual teacher, the one who says; "*I am going to tell you lies, I am going to be hate and fear – are you going to wake up and remember who, you are? Who are you going to choose to be?*"

To be who we truly are – beings of love and light we need to heal our minds so we do not believe the lies based on fear, based on the thoughts – there is not enough, we are not enough, someone is out to get us, we are abandoned and alone, it's pointless. We must love more, and heal all the parts of us, which have been, and will continue to be, revealed to us as scenarios in our life play out.

For the rest of that morning on, I surrounded myself with love and ate the food that my inner child needed, I gave and received hugs and had beautiful conversations with strong women full of love, and as the day progressed I felt only love.

This day also happened to be my first day as a new presenter at our local community radio station, Radio Saltire. Together, with a dear friend, we ran a show called Good Vibrations. The day before our first show we chatted about the playlist in relation to the election. We were not allowed to voice our political views, so the song I decided to play as a love message, no matter the result, was 'Firework' by Katy Perry. Regardless of how people in America voted, or what we feel about Trump's policies and beliefs, I wanted to play a song which would spark the belief that we do, in fact, hold the power which lives deep inside us.

As it turned out, due to the result, this song was an even better choice than I'd anticipated. It was a song to raise my vibration and for anyone else who felt the same as me. I believe it will remind us we need to be in the total opposite energy of that election campaign. We need to be love, not hate. We need to tell the truth, not lies. We need to lean on the divinity inside of us, not on the words of those outside us. We need to let ourselves be seen, not hide behind any labels or comparisons. We need to shine our light and step into the darkest parts of ourselves. We need to heal those parts and bring them home too.

If we let our divinity guide us, others will do the same – that's the ripple effect we want to create. As I write, in November 2018, spiritual teacher and author Marianne Williamson is currently in the early stages of considering running for President as the Democratic candidate in 2020. Whether she runs or not is being determined by a worldwide tsunami of Divinity. When I heard this news, my whole body tingled – her mantra is so empowering; *"Love is what we are born with, fear is what we learn here. Choose love over fear – it's your birthright!"*

28

Your gremlins don't live in nature

Every year, thousands upon thousands of holidaymakers find their way to the coastal town of North Berwick where I live. It is as if the sea pulls them there. It certainly pulled me there, almost 14 years ago.

One thing I discovered when I began living by the sea, is that I always felt better after time out in nature. It was living here that encouraged me to take up running and sea swimming, and both of these have played a huge part in healing my psyche. I also noticed that if I took my children to the beach – they would come alive and play together well, no fights happened in nature!

Simply put, our gremlins don't live in nature, so any time spent here, is less time spent with them. With increasing numbers of people being diagnosed with stress, depression and anxiety, I think one of the key solutions is to spend time in nature. Whether it's on the beach, in the water, in the woods or up a mountain, there is something powerful about being in a high vibrational environment.

Five days before I became a patient at the Priory I'd been for a run on the beach with my dog Seaweed. I was very aware that something was not okay with my state of mind and yet, at the same time, I felt so sure I was being guided through it all. I vividly remember stopping in one of the little bays and feeling this overwhelming urge to go for a swim. I hesitated, because I was afraid, perhaps I wouldn't come back, because life was feeling all too much. Being a witness to such dark thoughts was my divine self – I know she was taking me to nature so I could feel her more. I felt a calmness rise inside and I felt sure my intentions were good, so I took off my trainers and socks and spoke – semi-joking – to my dog *"Will you come in with me Seaweed? I'm a bit scared I might not come back."* Without hesitation she headed to the water's edge and we stepped into the Scottish sea together. As I fully submerged I felt all the tension, doubt and fear disappear. I lay on my back and screamed with joy as tears of relief rolled down my face. I learnt in that moment that I can trust myself, far more than my inner gremlins, would have me believe.

Stepping out of the water, I experienced what I can only now describe as a flash forward in time, I felt stronger and more certain in my body. I was incredibly calm, I knew I was to become a writer and that I would write about love and cherishing all parts of ourselves. It became crystal clear that my daughter needed me to love and cherish all parts of myself, for her, and for all those whom I loved. This was all that mattered. I walked back, barefoot, from the beach with a feeling of peace surging through every fibre of my being. I had no idea everything was about to collapse around me and within 48 hours I would be admitted to the Priory as doctors thought I was experiencing a manic episode. I am eternally grateful that nature pulled me back into her arms – things were firmly in motion and could not be undone.

During my stay in the Priory I was shocked at how disconnected from nature the building was. Deep down I knew the healing effects of being in the sea and the woods – I felt that Mother Nature had finally gotten through to me and more than anything I needed rest and time in nature. So spending six weeks in this closed-off environment was one of the hardest parts of my stay.

A mantra that is close to my heart is 'everything that is happening is happening for you' and so with my new-found connection to Source I chose to trust that there was an important reason I was in this environment. I feel I was there, in part, to see how the mental health care system needs to change – how it needs to work with mother nature to let her raise the vibrational energy of those who were feeling the pain of being a human on earth. This is why The Barefoot Sanctuary and the type of coaching I offer now exists – all led by the high vibrational healing effects of nature. In fact the location of The Barefoot Sanctuary was completely influenced by this. I remember being excited about the building's potential, but a familiar tight feeling in my chest surprised me. I told the landlord's representatives that something felt a bit unsure in my body and I was going to climb the Law, with my dog Seaweed and I'd get back to them. Admitting this is something I would never have done before. It was only when I got to the top of the Law, feeling much lighter in my body that I remembered I needed to decide on if I was going ahead with the building. There is an incredible view over the entire town from the top and as I looked down, my gaze was drawn immediately to the building in question. I remember laughing out loud. It was as if the building was smiling and waving up at me. I realised immediately that Mother Nature wanted me to understand the connection between her and this building. Nature was going to be a major part of the energy of The Barefoot Sanctuary. It is one of the most frequent things people comment on – the feel-good feeling within the building.

Things have since moved on in mental health but the connection of our mental health, physical health and spiritual health are the crux of it all. My first room in the Priory had a beautiful tree outside its window, and it was so peaceful to look at. But if I came out of my room, to the staff station, it was dark and totally devoid of such peace. After a day, or two, I started to leave my door deliberately wide-open so the staff saw daylight and felt the healing effects from this tree. And there were certain staff members, who I know this made a big difference to. If just having a view of nature can make such a big difference – imagine the difference full immersion regularly in nature could make to your life.

I no longer experience stress or anxiety in the way I used to. And yes, whilst I went through some traditional therapy, without nature and its powerful medicine, life would feel very different. It's time to really let nature play its part.

29

What is effortless to you is priceless to somebody else

"Hi Bernie, you write about, 'your ness' frequently in your posts, but I'm not fully sure what you mean or how I recognise it? Please can you explain this to me?"

This was a question asked by one of my blog readers. It was such a great question, because my understanding of the word 'ness' has continued to evolve and grow.

I still understand 'ness' as our God-ness, in the form of human-ness, without judgement, without labels. Once we open ourselves up to the possibility that we are loved unconditionally by Source, GOD, and more importantly, that Source needs nothing from us, then we are free to just be.

However, I realised, even with my new perspective, I was still, judging and diminishing all that I felt. More layers to peel – forever more.

I began using the term 'ness' in 2010 during the period of my life that I call my awakening. As the puzzle pieces of my life were coming together, it may have appeared on the outside, that I was actually falling apart. The American comedy film *'You, Me and Dupree'* made a lot of sense during this time. As Carl, the main character discovers, your ness is what flows through you, and at first you won't even be aware of it, it just does. People who, love and like you, do so because they value your ness and are enriched by it. Without even trying, you are just being yourself, and by feeding, honouring and owning your ness your life feels more fun, more joyful and effortless. Remember what is effortless to you is priceless to somebody else.

Your ness will shine when you allow the essence of love to flow through you. When you do, when you are fully in the present and not reacting to your conditioning, then it is the GOD in you running the show, so to speak. It is what other people see and love about you – a random act of kindness, a loving smile, fully listening as someone speaks. It is also the energy that vibrates out of your personality, your fiery-ness, your blunt-ness, your chatty-ness, and your direct-ness. As you awaken, you'll get a glimpse of what other people are drawn to and see, and you'll become conscious of it. But your ness is not static. There's more of you to come.

In 2010, I remember very clearly telling myself, and others that I had lost my ness and if I could; *"just be Bernie"* everything would be okay. By this I meant 'a strong confident Bernie' yet I baled out of tricky situations believing that my scared-ness, childish-ness or feelings of weakness were too dominant and wrong. I had yet to understand that allowing myself to feel these emotions every time and present whichever ness was flowing, was where peace lay and from this I would feel whole. I would have to keep repeating it, as life would constantly throw me opportunities to show up fully.

As another layer was revealed, it became clear, that I had only remembered and understood part of the bigger picture as, of course, our ness isn't just the smiling, shiny, happy confident part of ourselves, it's all of us.

We are born whole and complete, we are literally Love, but we are also spiritual beings on earth, and we learn and absorb feelings and beliefs that create our beliefs about the human experience. These are not necessarily true but there is value in feeling them.

Your ness is like the vast ocean – not containable or rigid, there is ebb and flow, there are gigantic, powerful and seemingly destructive storms, yet there are also still, calm waters, all to be experienced, all to be felt. These are part of your human experience and by allowing yourself to feel these emotions, the storms return to calm, equilibrium is restored and peacefulness is experienced once more.

What ever you resist persists

I am very curious and this comes in handy when looking at what's going on inside of me. With this, came the realisation, of how annoyed I became when people said; *"Bernie is nice"*. I was spotting a pattern – nice little girl, nice pupil, nice woman, nice, nice, nice. But, whilst I can be nice, back then, I didn't always feel nice. In fact I had mean thoughts, frustrations, anger, rage at times and I felt that if I showed anything other than nice, I would be rejected and condemned. I felt that others would not like me and I wasn't letting myself be. It was such a conditioned fight or flight response. It wasn't until I realised that keeping a lid on things means no one can really get close to you, and you are denying yourself the opportunity to get the thing you crave so much, true connection. This is a vicious cycle, which only affirms the lie that you are not loveable.

The reason we can be reluctant to allow all parts of ourselves to be ourselves, is because we are taught from a very young age and it is still taught in all religions today, that we have to love a God that is great and mighty. We are taught we have to earn his love, fear his judgement and this has penetrated the psyche of so many, across all religions and even those who don't believe in 'said God' have been affected by it. It is, therefore, no wonder that denial and pretence feel a lot safer in the game of conditional love.

Thankfully, this denial and pretence finally started to feel very uncomfortable to me, and the beautiful truth about my GOD was soon to be revealed. And of course, no one is meant to be nice all the time. In my case, some people along my 'nice' journey didn't experience nice Bernie at all, and they were my greatest guides and teachers. Those closest to us, our loved ones and family are in this category, as we often feel safer to show more of ourselves to these people. Although it was a relief to reveal other emotions to my teachers and guides, it did not sit well with me as a people-pleaser that people might think of me as 'not nice'. Consider the phrase; "Oh yeah, now they're showing their true colours!"

I was starting to get a sense that there was something bigger going on in this emotional feedback system and I became even more curious as to why we show up differently to different people. Why do some people draw out the best of us, and others seemingly the worst? I felt sure there had to be a connection between when we are unhappy and insecure, or experiencing stress and anxiety, and lashing out in ways that make us feel terrible afterwards.

I remember, one time, saying to my son when he was expressing grumpy-ness; *"Hey what's up? That's not like you!"* Almost as soon as the words left my mouth I realised I'd put him in a box, and I changed tack. I allowed him to be, and told him he could and should feel how he was feeling – his behaviour shifted pretty quickly into a better place, because he was allowed to express how he'd been feeling. It reminded me of a situation years earlier when one of my work colleagues said to me; *"I was really surprised when you said that, it's so not like you"*.

But the truth is, as human beings we feel a huge range of things – we may be open about them or we may bury them – it's an either or. If we normally bury what we feel, it will appear out of character to those who think they know us, when another form of 'ness' shows up. Unknowingly, I was putting my son into a very restrictive box too. We have to feel the darkness, experience it, so we remember that we are love, we are the light. Everything happens so we wake up to love and accept all of who we are. Emotions are simply a feedback mechanism, guiding us back to our experience of wholeness. It is vital for our sake and those in our world that we don't shut any of them down.

The best piece of wisdom I have been given is; *"What other people think of you, is none of your business."* This is integral to you honouring your ness. It's the message I am now sharing with my children, so they will continue to allow themselves to show up unlimited. It's what we all need to remember on a daily basis.

Take another moment to think about what personality or emotional labels are defining you, but don't serve you anymore – that restrict your growth and stifle your sense of joy? What feels too rigid and unsustainable? Think about how differently you would show up if you set yourself free from the labels, other people might have for you, or if you let go of what other people expect from you or think about you.

In our own observations we may have been contained or we might have contained someone. As, I did with my son and how I felt contained by the label of 'nice'. That is when we are not allowing ness to just be, to just flow. This is when we send out, unknowingly perhaps, to ourselves and to others conditional love signals. It's time we took ourselves and others out of the boxes, stopped the labels – it's time we realised that we are all human beings, we are all emotional but we are also so much more.

Honouring our ness is the golden gateway home but we are only able to access this, and let it lead us, if we allow ourselves to feel all that we feel when we feel it. By doing so, we are also able to let others feel what they need to. Your ness is so special because it allows you to be you – the perfect imperfect human being.

For me, turning 50, allowed me to lean back to another part of my ness – my 'Bernadette-ness' as I once again started to use my full name. For years I consciously and unconsciously rejected the parts of me called Bernadette – choosing to be know as Bernie. I realised to truly lean into being all of me I needed to embrace the name I chose for myself before I came onto this earth. What about you? What parts of your past are you still rejecting? Boring, straight, nice, stupid, weak, ugly, noisy, naive? Dust them down. They truly are your greatest gifts.

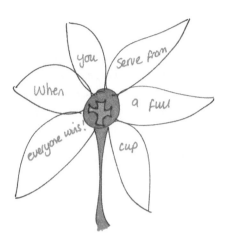

30

When you serve from a full cup everyone wins

One of the myths, which I believe causes a lot of suffering, is the belief that we need to be selfless. So often in my childhood I heard praise for those that were 'selfless till the end'. People are admired for it – sainted for it. I cannot tell you the number of times I was told to be more like my namesake, Saint Bernadette. Like anything in life, without knowing all the details about what was happening within that person at the time, the act might not have felt selfless at all. The person might have felt deep joy in their giving – right to the end. In fact, they might have actually been experiencing 'oneness'. However those trying to emulate the same behaviour, may not experience the same joyful experience, so they end up feeling resentful, burnt out and in some cases very ill – a very different ending.

What is the difference? Those who serve joyfully are serving with a full cup –so full, it's overflowing. It's easy and joyful. Even those who might sacrifice their lives will have done so from a full cup, connected to the source of all love, the Divine. They will have felt no separation – the feeling of oneness was so strong.

The responsibility each of us has, in this life, is keeping that cup so full it's overflowing. We need to know ourselves so well, that we pay attention to the feedback from our bodies. We need to learn what drains us rapidly and what restores us sustainably.

What is going on with our planet is connected to what is going on within each and every human. And just like the planet can, and will, joyfully serve us from a full cup, she will not be able to sustain this if her resources are depleted beyond repair. If each of us starts to take responsibility for the natural resources inside us, our external world resource will shift too. We will feel oneness with the planet and others on it.

Throughout my time working with people and their energy levels – I have seen many people serving with far-from-full cups, and I realise I was once the same. I had a glimpse of our actual 'oneness' in 2010 and crucially my first lesson, if I was to serve this world in the way I believe I am meant to, was to ensure I stay connected to the Source that keeps my cup overflowing. I learned that if I stay within my joy, my cup is overflowing and serving is almost effortless. An important indication of whether we are genuinely serving from a full cup is whether we feel energised or drained, and in my experience, there is no exception. Giving yourself permission to shine is sometimes saying no – especially when you realise your cup isn't as full as it needs to be. Think back to times when you have felt more drained or more energised – that is your clue.

With practice and with daily devotion we may at some point understand that we never have to leave the Source of our sustenance and we have the ability to be forever attached to the main supply. But let's face it, we are human, we will wander off on adventures, unconsciously disconnecting from Source, and in that moment, we are no longer full but running on reserves. This can only last so long before we are running on empty. It often takes the running-on-empty experience for us to realise we have become disconnected from Source. Once we have remembered our true Source it becomes easier – the goal is living in the full experience now. This is, indeed, a noble goal because if you achieve this, you are loving and cherishing the human, that you are – that is personal responsibility, that is self-love. And self-love is the noblest, most Godly ambition of them all.

SECTION TWO

See your future

SEE YOUR FUTURE

If you could see your future
through my eyes you would laugh.
You would giggle jump up and down,
there would be no place for a frown.

If you could see your future
with eyes free to be,
you just might discover,
that you're amazing to me.

What you really desire
is hidden deep inside,
let me help you find it,
let me help you thrive.

Are you being honest with the universe?

A couple of years ago I spent a week in Mallorca on a 'girls trip'. I had been here once before with my husband when we were expecting our first child. I remember how much I loved the place, which was a complete surprise as my perception of this island had been totally skewed.

Why was it so skewed? Because for me, it was easier and less painful to just dislike the idea of Mallorca. Two holidays to this island had previously eluded me – once as a child and then as a teenager. As a child I had wanted to visit with my childhood friend and her parents and then as a teenager, with two school friends. But neither happened and I buried my feelings of rejection and disappointment.

It is a human trait, when we are jealous of something – something we secretly desire – we convince ourselves it's not worth experiencing and we trash it. I criticised everything about Mallorca throughout my twenties. However, my view of Mallorca was altered, when in my early thirties, I happily, although still somewhat skeptically, stepped on a plane and visited this gorgeous island. Since then, it has held a special place in my heart, and serves as a great reminder of how wrong our minds can be and encourages me to discover what other hidden limiting beliefs I might have.

This 'girls trip' was a trip with a difference, because it was about dreaming, planning and creating for the future – as we were there primarily to write. If you had told my disappointed 12 and 18-year-old selves that I was to become a spiritual guide and coach and would be spending a creative week with an American-born Theta Healer, Jennifer Main and Scottish-born Compassionate Business Coach, Alisoun Mackenzie on the island of Mallorca – they would have been blown away. I think my reaction would have been along the lines of; "*Oh my God* (huge grin) *Really? No way – is that how my life will be? Are you really telling me the truth?*"

I may have even cried – okay, hands up I know I would have cried. I can feel the tears now as I write. I'm smiling and being healed by the thought of my 12-year old-year self, beaming. I had forgotten she could do that.

Why am I telling you this? Because each and every one of us has desires, desires which run deep but also desires which may have been hidden away. Desires which have been ignored and forgotten and those we might even scoff at, when they are mirrored back to us, through the lives of others. We are so often unaware of what is actually going on, right under our noses – of the gifts we actually have – the desires inside of us bursting to come out.

My secret desire as a child and then as young woman was to lead a creative life. To have meaningful, connected and loving conversations; To write and read beautiful words; To travel and to feel joy; To create beautiful things and lead an interesting, joyful, rich life. But somewhere along the way I suppressed these desires, thought them unachievable and, even worse, considered my already beautiful, interesting life too dull and boring. Why? Plain and simply, because I wasn't present, I was wishing I was someone else, I was wishing myself away.

"*You wished yourself away, and with that so much more. You doubt your value. Do not run from who you are.*"– Aslan to Lucy, 'Chronicles of Narnia: Voyage of the Dawn Treader.'

In the last eight years, many parts of my external life have not seen a lot of change, yet internally – how I view myself and experience life has radically changed. By being much more present I am able to practise loving and cherishing all that I am. I'm actually able to experience life how the Universe has always seen it – a beautiful, magical, creative life. In the past I would not have dared voice the desires of my soul, I was under the illusion it would be too painful. But that's all it was – an illusion.

Our ordinary stories are so rich and full of love, and the Universe is listening to all of our feelings – if we are brave enough to be honest about how we feel she will show us the way forward. Three times yearly I tune in, even more diligently, to how I feel in that particular moment and how I would like to feel, going forward in my life. As part of a workshop I run – See Your Future – I discover my core soul desires. I discover three words, which I will lean into, and use as verbs. I use them to make my decisions for the next four months until I revisit the process again. Please don't underestimate the power you have inside you and around you, to do what you came here to do. If you can start to be honest with yourself and the Universe, about who you truly are, and how you truly want to feel, your life will feel transformed. Remember your desires will not happen without action on your part too, but inspired action makes all the difference and sharing it with others, as we do in these workshops, starts the momentum. Share your dreams and be ready to take action. No one but you can give you permission to live your secretly desired life.

Where are you really trying to get to?

One day, while out walking on the beach with my two spaniels, Seaweed and Scout, I came across a scene, which was familiar to me, from my days as parent of toddlers.

A grandmother and her daughter were in the middle of lifting a buggy with two toddlers, over rocks, to get to the next part of the beach. Believe me it is a challenge for two people. I remember the team effort required when my husband and I had to do it, over the same spot, on our family beach walks. I felt for them as they tried to navigate their way across this rocky part of the coastline.

We got chatting as we navigated the rocks together. It became clear they were unsure of where they were actually heading, as we were moving away from the town centre. I asked; *"Where are you trying to get to?"* The Grandmother replied wearily; *"We are looking for the shops and to get something to eat."* I smiled and, with much empathy, said; *"Ah, I see, the thing is, the shops and cafes are back the way you came. You're actually moving away from them."*

As I gave directions back to town and recommendations of where to eat, they realised they had, unknowingly, headed off completely the wrong way – they had taken many steps but in the opposite direction. I could feel their desire to sit down for lunch and to potter in the shops. I could feel the deep internal sigh as they realised they had moved unnecessarily far away from what they set out to achieve, when they had boarded the train to North Berwick. No wonder it felt like such an effort lifting the buggy over the rocks, they did not need to be there in the first place. With a definite destination in mind and directions as to how to get there, they headed off in pursuit of the high street.

Later that afternoon, I caught a glimpse of them heading back to the train station – mission achieved. If we don't know where we are trying to get to, how do we get there? And if we don't recognise where we are, at each stage of our journey, how do we know the steps we are taking are leading us towards where we want to be? Or as in the case of that family – are they leading us in the completely opposite direction?

Nine years ago I realised the place I wanted to get to, was a place of peace inside me. So wherever I was, I knew I was there for the right reasons. From that place, whatever I encountered along the way, I would be equipped to deal with, as long as I kept my focus on how I wanted it to feel.

The life I have now is the future I started to visualise nine years ago, prior to that, it felt unreachable. Remember – discontent is the first necessity of progress. In the case of the family in my story, their discontent manifested whilst trying to traverse rocks carrying a buggy. Until that point, they had unknowingly been going in the wrong direction. It's only, when it became uncomfortable, and they thought about what they really wanted, that real progress followed.

In the past, I couldn't admit to myself, or others, what my desires actually looked like, so I wasn't honest about them. Even when I felt mild discontent, the direction I needed to take eluded me, and so life had to become really uncomfortable.

If we are honest with ourselves and with others, we will have all the help and guidance we need. Once we know where we are trying to get to, the rest will take care of itself. The Universe is tuned into our desires, so the more we fine-tune them, the more it will feel like magic is happening. This is not necessarily easy to do. For a multitude of reasons we bury the truth about what we really want, so we genuinely don't know. However, our internal compass knows!

You have and are your own internal compass

Have a think about where you are trying to get to? It may look very different from the landscape currently surrounding you. But with an idea of how you would like it to feel, it will come into view and there you will be.

You might think you want a new relationship, but what you really want is the freedom to be you. Give yourself permission to take steps towards being more you.

You might think you want to be liked, but what you really want, is to like being you? Focus on what you like about you and lean into that more.

Maybe you think you would like to be rich, but what you really want is to feel abundant? Start paying attention to all that feels rich and is abundant in your life. Write down the things you can appreciate today and watch your feeling of abundance grow.

Tune into your desires, take inspired action and let the Universe take care of the rest.

32

Don't stay in the past you won't find me there

Without a doubt, this is one of the most powerful messages the Divine has for us. Largely, our human suffering is caused by not being totally present. It is no surprise to me that I could not hear Divine's guidance, because for many years I was stuck in my head and my head was often in the past. I would replay scenarios in my head – have revised pretend conversations with people I was in conflict with, or felt obligated to – conversations that were never going to happen. Psychologists call this 'ruminating'. This takes up so much of our precious creative energy and it is in the realm of the victim mindset – it is far from the mindset of the Divine.

The Divine can help us heal the past and visualise the future. But this will only happen when we are fully present – connected to our body – and then we can feel the Divine presence within. Ruminating is like a fog, which stops the clarity, preventing a solid connection. We always tend to ruminate about the past. *"If I had said this"* or *"If I had done that"* and *"If only that hadn't happened"*. Things that didn't happen, words that were said or not said, cannot be undone and we need to make peace with this. We need to let go of things that are no longer open to us; business opportunities, job opportunities, relationships – if we stay focusing on them, holding onto something which has gone – we are far from present. If we stay in the past, we are not truly living, as the Divine only resides in the here and now. In truth, there is no past, there is no future, there is only now.

It can be difficult to believe that things can be salvaged, that you can make things that have broken, work. But, in my experience, it was only when I totally let go of the past and moved into the present that, the real direction of my life became obvious. If I look back at the journal I wrote, during my stay at the Priory, I still believed my involvement with someone else's start up business, could continue and every time I focused on this, I was missing the clues to the life that lay ahead of me. A new life as a coach and writer, led with Divine intention.

Take a moment and come back into present as often as you can. Try to do this as much as possible or even for a few minutes every day. You will, of course, catch yourself in the past, but day-by-day with practice, you will realise you are living life more divinely in the here and now, no matter what is going on around you. Plus, you can deal with life as the complete, present-minded human being you are. It can help, if you put up signs in the bathroom, on your desk or on the fridge saying; *"I'm Here Now"*. We need to coach our mind to stay in the present, make it easier by using cues. The following words are a short, yet powerful prayer; *"I am ready and willing to let go of the past – thank you for healing the parts of me stuck there. I am ready and willing to be divinely guided by you in the here and now, forever more. Amen"*

33

You are worthy of the life you dream of

Part of my work involves taking clients on a guided journey – visualising their dream life. I am fully aware that visualisation alone is not going to get people the life they desire. However if you can dream of a life, it means you are on a deeper level, a match to it. We often confuse how we want to feel with material things. When we are truly dreaming it's all about how we want to feel. We might think we want the fancy job or flash car, because then we might feel important or successful. Yet the reality is, they are never enough, because we have to feel enough on the inside first.

After graduating from university, I went into the business world and no matter how many material possessions I accumulated, it never felt enough. I now realise I pursued better labels because of the belief, that surely the next one would make me feel better, but none of them ever did. Because none of them truly can – there is not one label, on this earth, that can define who you are.

Not once did I dream about being a Sales Director and yet at the age of 29, I was, at least to the outside world, successful and living a dream life with an impressive title, a company car and a big monthly pay check. And then again at 37 – a full-time mother of two adorable children, a big house and a loving husband. But in both cases, there was one common thread – a deep feeling of loneliness and it not feeling enough – still not truly present.

It was only when I woke to the bigger reality – I had always been enough – that I experienced the joy a glimpse of eternity gives you. I remembered what my little two-year-old self's dreams had really been about, and I was able to work on letting go of the limiting beliefs that would stop me from dreaming as freely as I had then. Finally, I was able to see what was right with my life and be more present in it and I realised this is what my dreams were actually about. My ability to be fully present in my body is why I enjoy taking people on these guided journeys so much, but we have to be connected to that divinity first.

If you find that dreaming is difficult, even the mention of it makes you feel uncomfortable then an inner dialogue is still going on in your mind, trying to keep you small, trying to even keep you safe, and that's okay. But you are worthy of the life you used to dream of, and reconnecting with that feeling by reconnecting with your divinity – your own North Star – will make all the difference.

34

You are your own North Star

'Finding Your Own North Star' by bestselling author and life coach Martha Beck was published in 2003. By the time I discovered her work in 2012 I was well on my way to becoming a coach, having finally began to trust my internal wisdom as my North Star. During this time I was looking for examples of coaches who trusted their intuition rather than coaching modalities and guided by my inner wise self, Martha appeared as if magically! Martha is such an inspiration to me, and millions of others, because she trusted her intuition at a crucial decision making point of her life.

> *"There comes a point in our lives when we can only make a significant decision based on what feels right – this is when we finally discover our North Star."* – Martha Beck.

Our fascination with the stars is as long as time itself. Early sailors learnt to navigate by the stars as they travelled the globe, plotting them with incredible precision. The North Star, as it is known in the Northern Hemisphere, is simple to find in the right conditions, namely a clear still night. It sits at the top right of the star constellation we know as The Plough. It is so named because it sits directly above the North Pole and, interestingly, it doesn't move from that spot as other stars do. Sailors would seek out the North Star so they could effortlessly steer their course correctly.

Today, millions of people look to the stars for guidance, on a daily basis, as they navigate through modern life. But many people do not realise that the star guidance we actually need to follow is not in the external sky, but in our internal nightscape. The truth is, following it isn't the easiest route, its scary – sometimes terrifying – but it's the only way we will ever be truly satisfied and truly happy.

Our internal wisdom, our intuition, reveals where we truly are on our journey. Like the sailors who recognised the importance of the North Star, for our internal voyage we must rely on the same recognition. It takes moments of stillness to discover it, yet it is always in the same spot deep inside us – it is a constant.

That night in July 2010 as I became a brilliant ball of light, it was as if I was alone in the clearest of night skies. Yet, I finally knew where to look forever more – my very own North Star had been hidden inside me, it had been there constantly. This wisdom, this guidance is within each and every one of us. It's our true north and it will be unique to each and every one of us, we are all on our own voyage of discovery.

Start searching inside yourself, allow yourself to be still. Then allow the clouds – the unhelpful thoughts and opinions and other bright distractions – to float by. With each breath you take, focus northwards and the internal vision will become clear. Your inner guidance will shine brightly and even though it's scary, following it will be as necessary for you as it was for those courageous sailors.

35

Follow your own yellow brick road

I vividly remember the joy of watching the 'Wizard of Oz' for the first time, my eyes agog when Dorothy arrived in the colourful Oz.

I believe we each have our own yellow brick road. The permission to shine, we seek, is deeply connected to our ability to see and follow our own yellow brick road. A golden pathway is in place to help us evolve and experience a more meaningful life. It may not always look golden but it ultimately leads to gold.

What if our own yellow brick road is the intuitive pathway – a way of living that leans solely on our intuition? A way of living where, you journey with courage, an open heart and using your intuitive intelligence – just as Dorothy and her three travelling companions did. A way of living that is unlimited and far more colourful and magical. A way of living which is possible for us all – and one which many amongst us are already living.

What if your inner wise self is laying the bricks for you in the exact place you need to be, to experience all of who you are? To reveal all, of who you are? What if everything you meet on your yellow brick road is perfectly orchestrated for you – so you experience exactly what you need to experience. What if your inner wise self communicates through your body to you, her yes and her no?

Often we might be so busy focusing on someone else's journey, envying their life path, that, we don't even notice we are on our very own yellow brick road, and despite the continual laying of bricks our inner guidance system is ignored. We might feel lost and no matter how brightly the sun shines on our own pathway we fail to see it, because we are focused on someone else's.

In the year before my stay in the Priory I was so busy desiring someone else's path, I missed that I was wearing my very own pair of ruby slippers and had a clear path of my own, laid right out in front of me. The period from July 2009 to July 2010, when I look back, seems almost surreal. I was anxious most of the time, yet a voice deep inside was trying to get through. It was only when, on a few occasions that love overrode fear, that I really started to notice the difference and become curious about what my body was trying to tell me.

It was at this time, one Friday morning, as I was sitting in a local coffee shop; there was a group of mums laughing and chatting, and suddenly I felt a feeling of peace inside me and I knew, that at this moment, I was exactly where I was meant to be. It was such a contrast to how I'd felt before, but I was so present and it made me realise that I hadn't been truly present for a long time. This little moment was a 'yes' moment.

A few weeks later, before getting into my car to drive to a meeting I experienced a very strong 'no' moment. Nothing had felt right that morning, I was indecisive about what to wear and I was flustered, which resulted in spilling coffee over my computer. I had also underestimated how long it would take me to drive to the meeting and my anxiety peaked. My chest became really tight and a dark, suicidal thought flashed momentarily through my mind. This really scared me and the drive was one of the scariest I have ever taken in my life. I repeatedly got lost trying to navigate roads I knew and had driven often, and I felt sure I was at risk of driving my car off the road. Then, something inside me became very still and a quiet thought of; "*call them*" popped up and, then again; "*call them and say you will be late – its okay.*" They, of course, couldn't have been nicer and the meeting went well, but I was left very shaken and realised something definitely was not right with my state of mind. But I also knew that, inside me was a voice, which maybe knew how I could get back on the right path. It took another type of crash, an emotional crash, just a few weeks later to help me wake up to the realisation, that my life was as technicolour as the world of Oz. But it doesn't have to be that way for you there is an easier way to stay on your own path.

So how does our yellow brick road become more visible?

We have a multitude of muscles and it only takes some new or different exercise to reveal that these muscles have not been used for a long time. Yet they have been there all along. The same applies to our intuition. We have deep layers of intuitive muscle, but we have to use them daily and in new ways, to really excel as an intuitive traveller. It is in this daily commitment to use our intuitive muscle that we discover our yellow brick road has been there all along – our life feels more magical and colourful.

In practical terms this starts with the smallest of decisions on a daily basis and I mean small. What do you really want to eat or drink, who do you really want to spend time with, what clothes feel nice today? In fact, all decisions you make throughout your day can be intuitively made rather than on autopilot. You start to rediscover what you personally prefer and you start to hear a guidance coming from inside, just by pausing and letting your body speak to you. To experience the beauty of the yellow brick road you must tune into your body and allow it to guide you. Tuning into our preferences in the little things will reveal the bigger things which lead us to the magical life planted deep inside of us from the beginning. We learn to step forward with our intuitive preferences and suddenly the yellow brick road becomes clearer. We need to trust what our yes feels like, and what our no feels like. The body is always telling us, we just need to listen.

Now it's over to you – go hand-in-hand with courage and an open heart and discover you can intuitively trust your very own yellow brick road.

36

When you are too close to the elephant all you see is grey

I've known this quote for all of my adult life and it never gets old. But all too often, I am reminded that 'knowing' something is one thing – putting it into action is quite another. Lights, camera, action is never truer than in the creation of our own precious life, and if things are looking a bit dull, chances are we are just too close to something and we have lost sight of its magnificence.

We need to take a step back and see it for all its glory. One day I was chatting with a young woman, who is courageous and boldly creative, about this expression. She'd not heard it before, and as we talked, she saw how having a weeks holiday from her new life, in London, was helping her to see how incredible it actually was. In her day-to-day life she realised she was too close to it and wasn't able to see it in its full glory. She will return refreshed and renewed after taking some time away.

This was a powerful reminder, to me, that no matter how much we love our work or our daily life – without stepping back we do not get a change in perspective. Without moving ourselves, into a position, where we can see the bigger picture – we miss the benefit of perspective.

Think of an artist painting a huge canvas, or Michael Angelo painting the ceiling of the Sistine Chapel, they will have had to step back to take it all in. Not only to appreciate it, but to ensure that they were creating it the way their original vision intended.

We are the artists of our lives. We have had a grand vision from the beginning and, just like my young friend and famous artists, we all have to take those vital steps back, so we can remember the vision we held so clearly and adjust the depths and colours we all need to add to our lives.

People come to me for help in remembering their original vision because I have taken those steps back. (To be honest, I think, the Universe scooped me up, sat me on top of a mountain, and helped me see things much more clearly.) I am not too close to them, I have the ability to see them in their glory – it's not muddled with family history, associations or limiting beliefs, and I can help them see the beauty they have lost sight of. Once they see it they can continue to create their very own unique and beautiful masterpiece. I, too, still need constant help with this. I need to remember to step back so I can appreciate all that I am creating, and as any creative will tell you, that will never stop. Take one, or maybe several, steps back, go away for a few days, put down the project you are working on, move your position and you will change your perspective.

37

Focus on how you want things to be

Following the temporary bliss experienced in the Priory in 2010, I soon discovered that my thoughts and attention could switch randomly and even after my 'awakening' I didn't always create joyfully. I had a creative power but I still didn't like all I was creating.

I started working with Melody Fletcher, a wonderful energy coach, who helped me understand the law of attraction, so I could harness it effectively. Not one to beat around the bush, Melody was always direct; *"Bernie where is your focus?"* or *"Does it feel good to focus on that?"* Squirming, the penny would finally drop and I would well and truly feel, for that moment, reawakened.

With practice I began to see that if I focused on how I wanted things to be – that would come to pass. My relationship with my husband transformed and I experienced my children getting on far better. Problems which, would normally have me fretting for days, began to work out easily and effortlessly. The coaching clients I wanted to work with appeared, and it helped me create my 'See your Future Workshop'. All by shifting my focus. We all want things to feel better, but in the first instance we have to focus.

If you are skiing down a mountain, it isn't wise, to focus on where you don't want to go – you don't want to focus on falling down, unless, of course, you want to fall down. No, you want to focus on the next turn – or as in my early days of skiing, focus on the joy of getting to the bottom (for a hot chocolate). I can't tell you how many times I have skied, in my imagination, as a graceful skier in order to help my actual skiing. I began to realise other things could do with the same sort of focus.

There is a better way than worrying about how things are, there is a better way than focusing on the challenge, the hardship, the angst. Some might call it dreaming or fantasy, but another word for it is visualisation. There is so much evidence of its creative power. And inspirational people such as Jim Carrey, Andy Murray and Martin Luther King have been doing exactly this.

Focusing on how we want things to be is a lot more awesome than stewing on how things are. I am not talking about living in denial, I'm talking about paying attention to how you want to feel in the moments that you are able to, especially before you are in the real time situation. Believe me, you will be blown away by the changes.

Melody would tell me; *"Focus on how you want your relationship to be – see yourself communicating and laughing. Focus on how you want the experience to be – see yourself as if it's happening the way you would love it to happen."*

You are a powerful creator, either way, your focus will manifest – so why not make it beautiful? If something in your life isn't quite how you want it to be, put your attention on how you would really like things to be instead. Do this as frequently as you can and let the feeling of that desired reality sink in, and then keep moving forward.

Our focus really is powerful so let's harness it for the better.

Focus on your why and it will flow

When you focus on your 'why' things really do start to flow. Why is a powerful energy. When you knowingly or unknowingly connect with your why it activates your greatest strengths, and when these are in action it's pretty hard not to achieve what you want. Likewise, if you don't know your why – these strengths are not being used and things can feel stuck. It doesn't matter what your why is and as you grow it will shift and grow too. Your soul recognises the truth and, therefore, all of you is able to show up.

'Why' helped me achieve an important life goal. As a teenager my number one ambition was to become a student. I had no deep desire to study any particular course. I just wanted to be a student – in England. Why? Because I would go to a new country and meet new people, I loved the idea of learning about life, and I loved to party and being a student in the 80s and 90s was a sure way to achieve this goal. As the fourth of, originally, eight children I watched my three older siblings head off to Belfast and Cardiff, and this desire grew stronger and stronger.

I had (repeatedly) failed my maths O Level but, thankfully, I discovered Social Sciences courses didn't need maths and I liked the sound of them – Psychology, Philosophy and Social Policy. What I studied wasn't important I just wanted to be a student. So at 18-years-old I left

Ireland, for the very first time, and traveled by ferry to England to attend interviews at Loughbrough University and Trent Polytechnic in Nottingham.

I discovered I was not remotely keen on Loughbrough – it felt totally wrong for me. However, as we drove across the bridge to enter the city of Nottingham I felt like I was home. Something seemed to click deep inside; I knew I needed to be there, so I became super-focused.

One of my greatest strengths is enthusiasm and I'm pretty persuasive, especially when I feel passionately about something. And, I seemed to come into my own when I sat down with the Head of Applied Social Studies. When asked about my lack of life experience for the course, I replied; *"Look I do understand this, but sometimes you don't need to put your hand in the fire to realise it will hurt you. I have a sense of things and I am really good with people."* I was being interviewed for a Social Work Degree and as my interviewer was listening to me, he was looking at a letter I'd written saying why I would be a good social worker. To be honest, up until that point, I did not even know what a social worker was, I just wanted to go to college. There was a fair bit of creative writing in that letter – maybe a sign of the future to come?

The night before I'd been to a student ball – I've still not met anyone who has packed a ball dress to go to a college interview! I was well and truly hooked – this was why I wanted to go to Trent Poly. I showed up fully, and consequently I was offered a place.

However, a few months later, when exam results rolled in, I discovered I was a point short, which may have meant the end to my dream of becoming a student. I was initially devastated but then I got super busy. Because in the meantime, I had fallen in love with a boy I had met at the ball, so it became even more important for me to move mountains to make things happen. I phoned the Head of Applied Social Studies, he remembered me from the interview, and even though I was a point short, he took a chance on me. I also talked my way into halls of residence even though many of the places were supposedly gone. Why? Because being in halls of residence was paramount, as in my vision of being a student, this is where I was to be! Something inside me was driving the show and although I didn't understand it at the time, I now know it was where I was meant to be. Because in those halls of residence is where I met the ultimate love of my life, my husband. Yes the other boy didn't work out after all!

It truly doesn't matter what your why is – what matters is that your why is leading the way and in that energy you are unstoppable. The one caveat I would add – is make sure your why feels clean, in that it is about how you feel inside. It is not to get approval or validation from someone else, deep down that never feels right.

39

Nothing in this life is permanent

"What will make you feel better?" I believe this is one of the most important questions we can ever ask ourselves. As spiritual beings on a human adventure we came here to feel our way. Our time here isn't permanent, as we will move on to another adventure after this one. Death isn't permanent. We will emerge again and again. The futures are infinite. However, we are on this earth now, and we only ever experience things in the here and now, so when things are feeling tough we need to reassure our minds that the next now might not feel the same. Take a look at how this thought – *"Nothing in this life is permanent."* – could help you shift on a daily basis.

"None of my family and friends understand me – nothing in this life is permanent."

"My boss is horrible – nothing in this life is permanent."

"My jeans are too tight – nothing in this life is permanent."

"I hate my job – nothing in this life is permanent."

"I feel so ashamed – nothing in this life is permanent."

"I will never get over this – nothing in this life is permanent."

"I don't know what I'm doing – nothing in this life is permanent."

"I'm so broke – nothing in this life is permanent."

"I feel rubbish – nothing in this life is permanent."

When something bad happens, we can wrongly believe that things will never change and this belief causes so much suffering. But, actually, we have two choices – we can believe the thought, feed it and make sure that it lasts longer than it needs to, or we can focus on the thought; *"nothing in this life is permanent"*. Focus on what we can do, in the here and now, to feel better, then repeat and repeat.

Don't judge what it looks like. If you feel angry, it might mean standing on the top of a mountain and screaming your lungs out or punching some pillows. If you feel lethargic or ill, it might mean some tender loving care for yourself – taking a nap with a hot water bottle. If you feel afraid, it might mean sharing those fears with someone you trust or taking steps to do the thing that scares you, so fear doesn't win.

If I think back over the 50 years of my life, most of my suffering came from not realising that the things I was scared of, would pass. And that, the things I was ashamed of, I could forgive myself for and I would be free of that shame. That the anger I had inside me could be released, in a way that didn't hurt anyone else or be channeled into something far more productive. On the flip side, it helps me to realise, that we won't be here in this human form for ever, so I want to be present with it now, and not miss a single thing of being me. It also helps me realise that the good times roll, but they will continue to roll up and down and it's a reminder to not get overly attached to things staying the same. That to me feels exciting – being present with it all.

40

Let go of expectations and just play

The thing about playing is its intention is joyful, pure and fun loving. When we allow ourselves to play, our intentions line up with those of our Divine truth. Something emerges and something fun happens in the process. The vibration of play is very high and when our intentions are pure, we reach that higher vibration. It's almost like a perfect circle of energy is created in the essence of play.

Every time I sit down to write or paint with a set expectation – mush happens. It's only when I step out of the way and let go of any expectations and really play with the powerful intention of being as truthful as I can, that things flow. It's like a dance with the co-ordination already embedded in my soul. She knows it, and if I let her take the lead, magic starts to happen – an expanded version of who I am leads the way – the cant's and what if's fall away.

Remember, as a child, going to a neighbouring friend's house ringing their doorbell and saying the magical words; *"Are you coming out to play"*?

What if our inner wisdom is knocking on our door each and every day? Asking if we are willing to come out and play with her. She has no expectation, but her intention is loving, pure and very playful. When we do, it's like stepping out into the enchanted world of new possibilities. It's hope, enthusiasm and joy all wrapped up together. It's full of possibilities and it is asking us to show up and be that playful, light being she recognises we are.

How does this affect you right now? What expectations do you need to let go to give yourself permission to step back into the energy that we can all remember as children – the energy of play. We sabotage our time and energy by focusing on doing, not playing. Look at how much we achieved through play as children and how well we slept at night. Growing up doesn't have to mean throwing the baby out with the bath water. Some days we really have to say 'F**k it' to doing the misunderstood version of being grown up and allow that trusting playful magic back into our lives. The energy is there and we can still lean into it in adulthood. We will always be children of the Universe, so let's harness the power of play once again, and allow it to lead us into a more magical earth experience.

41

Your dreams are more supported than you know

At the very heart of any dream is a desire to feel something – a desire to feel seen, feel loved, feel supported, to feel free. The actual details of the dream are not nearly as relevant as the feeling locked inside them. Often we are unaware of the truth behind our dream, so it can look as though it is not happening. However, I believe the Universe is always listening and responding accordingly.

Emotional desires are always being listened to and the Universe is always responding – our job is to keep focusing on the dream and the feelings within it and trust it's okay to keep dreaming bigger. Perhaps you dream of becoming a writer, but, day after day, your fingers never make it to the keypad, instead you spend time with amazing words and stories locked in your head, missing the cues, signals and messages coming your way. Or perhaps you dream, of being free. Yet, redundancy after redundancy you apply for jobs, when perhaps the reason you keep being made redundant is your dream of freedom through travel. Instead of applying for yet another job maybe it's time to apply for a travel visa.

I dream of being free to be me and the essence of that dream is being able to live an authentic life – one where my family and I are open and honest with each other. A life where we enjoy supporting and loving each other whilst at the same time each of us are able to connect with other amazing souls from around this world. On a daily basis, I still need to take the action. I needed to spend hours writing this book and follow through with the conversations to make it happen. I needed to show up and pay attention to what was happening daily so I was writing with present awareness. And I needed to make time for those whom I love because they are the very reason why all of this matters. But my dreams won't happen without my action – we are the directors of our dreams.

Some of us will miss the daily cues – perhaps a redundancy, an illness, a breakdown or breakthrough. Any event, which finally forces us, to course correct, to fulfil a dream we sent out into the Universe a long time ago. This is hindsight, this is why you often hear people say; "*You know that was the best thing that actually ever happened to me.*"

Just because we haven't thought about our dreams for a while, doesn't mean they are forgotten. My current home in North Berwick is a perfect example of this. When I was 17-years-old I became friendly with a girl who lived in the small seaside town called Portstewart, a few miles from where I lived in Coleraine. Prior to this, I had many happy memories from summers spent, at Portstewart's beach and my Dad's golf club, where I watched golf tournaments, drank orange Fanta and ate buns. As a teenager, I remember visiting my friend's home in the heart of the town. The house itself was pretty quirky with a kitchen on the first floor opening out to a balcony with views of the sea. It felt so peaceful and amazing to be able to stare out to sea from the kitchen. I loved it and those feelings sparked a dream of one day living in a house over looking the sea. A few years ago we decided we needed to let go of our 'big house'. It felt really right to do this, despite the fact, that it was on a beautiful residential street with a huge garden. Some people thought we were mad to let go of such a prestigious property. After we moved into our current home and completed its refurbishment, I realised we had made my dream come true. We had created that funky home overlooking the bay, and only a few moments from the beach, high street and shops. Living this way had, for a long time, felt like a distant dream, but by following the Universal guidance it is now a daily reality.

Take a few moments to dust off the cobwebs covering your, seemingly, forgotten dream. Spend time believing and investing in your dream, making your dream shine so it is more visible to you and those who are ready to dance on the table with you too.

Honour your feelings and your vibration will rise

Inner work is to become familiar with the world within. It is to continue to grow and develop emotionally, psychologically, interpersonally, spiritually, and creatively. It is to tend to the wounds of the past, which are the inevitable result of living and loving, and to seek healing for them. For eight years, I have been consciously doing this – I was, of course, doing it unconsciously for even longer. I just didn't understand it, in the way that I do now. Knowing is only part of it.

Our feelings are there to help us dance through this matrix called life. They are key to harnessing positively the law of attraction. No feeling is less valuable, than another, none are superior, even if they vary in position on the vibrational (emotional) scale. The Emotional Guidance Scale from the Abraham-Hicks school of thought is a scale of our feelings and emotions, in sequence from our highest vibrational feelings to our lowest.

What we focus on makes all the difference – if we feel overwhelmed (11) but allow ourselves to do whatever will make us feel better this, we will shift to a level of hopefulness (6) fairly quickly.

For example, one Tuesday morning while writing this book, I was feeling incredibly overwhelmed. I didn't want to get out of bed, the 'shoulds' were rolling around my head and I could feel myself slipping downwards. I felt like a child, not wanting responsibility, I needed to be mothered. I gently asked myself what would make me feel better, the result, was to pull the covers over my head and curl up in a ball, a really tight ball. By surrendering to the feelings of overwhelm rather than batting them away, I instantly felt better. Within five minutes I was hot and irritated (10) and finally bored (8) and five minutes later I was feeling very hopeful (6) as I relaxed underneath a gloriously hot shower. My vibration continued to rise throughout the day and the things I had been feeling overwhelmed about I was able to take care of.

But, if instead of gently mothering myself, I would have continued to slip down the scale. Blame (15) would have come into play and I could have spiralled even further down to victimhood (22).

I have been up and down this scale many times – I have been my own worst enemy, which means I can recognise the emotions and, most importantly, I am no longer afraid of feeling any of these emotions. The five days leading up to my arrival at the Priory saw me experience all of these emotions which for years I tried to keep a lid on, thinking this was key to my survival. It is from this very experience, that I began to feel, that I began to write this book. Feeling all these emotions is how we actually thrive. We are able to make ourselves feel better, at any time, by loving and cherishing who, we are, and we do this by honouring our feelings.

Where do you feel on this scale today? And instead of giving yourself a hard time about it – gently ask yourself; *"Honey what would make you feel better?"*

Allow your inner self to be heard, ask again and again until your vibrations feel joyful once more. Joyfulness is our inherent nature – look at a baby and notice how quickly they go from sadness to joy. And, we can relearn how to return to our joy quicker than our minds would have us believe.

THE EMOTIONAL GUIDANCE SCALE

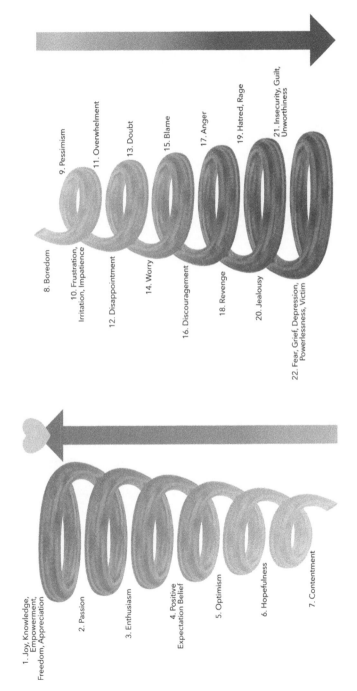

UPWARD SPIRAL

1. Joy, Knowledge, Empowerment, Freedom, Appreciation
2. Passion
3. Enthusiasm
4. Positive Expectation Belief
5. Optimism
6. Hopefulness
7. Contentment

DOWNWARD SPIRAL

8. Boredom
9. Pessimism
10. Frustration, Irritation, Impatience
11. Overwhelment
12. Disappointment
13. Doubt
14. Worry
15. Blame
16. Discouragement
17. Anger
18. Revenge
19. Hatred, Rage
20. Jealousy
21. Insecurity, Guilt, Unworthiness
22. Fear, Grief, Depression, Powerlessness, Victim

43

More than anything trust your inner wisdom

One day I was sitting at my desk looking out to sea, but unlike most days, I couldn't actually see it. If I had just teleported myself into the room from another time and place, and looked out of the window, I would have no idea that the sea was actually there – anything could have been behind that wall of fog.

But the fact remains I know the sea is there. Even though I couldn't see it, the knowledge was there. I had walked down to it, swam in it, seen it with my own eyes. I had experienced it, felt it, and I knew it from personal experience so no one could convince me otherwise. Seeing the fog, reminded me about trusting our own experiences and inner wisdom. That's how I've come to really know GOD.

As a child I struggled to accept someone else's definition of God. I needed to discover it for myself. To me GOD and the sea are one in the same. I listen to the sea the same way I listen to God – it guides me like GOD does. I look for signs and I still question. I trust what I'm feeling. It tells me when to come in and it tells me when not to, so I never dive in blindly any more.

Imagine this scenario. I have just teleported into the room, and I am looking out the window at a wall of fog. There is a person in the room with supposed knowledge, but in fact, they have not actually experienced the reality of the outside. Yet they say to me; *"Yes the sea is just there – it's a lovely bay and you can swim in it. Just dive right in, now, anywhere in the bay."* If I was to take their word for it and, literally, dive right in I might actually discover it is full of massive rocks, there are jellyfish or that there is a powerful riptide. I don't think it would be quite as nourishing as I'd hoped in fact it could prove disastrous.

But, if I was paying attention to my foolproof internal sat nav – my inner compass which, is actually my GOD (Glorious Onward Direction) mechanism, then blindly diving into this bay wouldn't feel right, if I was to be put in harms way. I would experience a sense of 'no', an off feeling in my body. This is the way GOD would easily communicate with me as I neared the water. That's the inner knowing – the point at which we get to choose. Maybe I need to go to a different spot in the bay, maybe it's a total no, or maybe I'll trust the feeling, which is suggesting I ask someone close by, who knows the area.

It is in the quiet moment of listening to our feelings, which enables us to prevent ourselves from going on blindly, because by pausing we tap into an eternal knowing and decide for ourselves. Ignoring the feeling of no, is blind faith and this does not necessarily feel good – we might actually feel abandoned.

Although, in truth, we have not been abandoned, we are not in the fog on our own. What we need is; to question, listen, act, feel and course-correct or continue forwards, then repeat. The human challenge is to wake up from our foggy and often limited perspective and to pay attention to our inner compass in order to gain a glorious perspective. Taking our power back comes from choosing to follow our inner GOD compass. And if we are not using our internal guidance it can feel like being lost at sea, lost in the fog.

We have all the inner guidance we need, right inside us, but we can only discover this for ourselves. It's not about taking someone's word for it – it's a deep knowing, from inside ourselves.

Exercise:

The following statements are designed to help your feedback mechanism into action. Say them to yourself and pay attention to how these words feel in your body.

If you get a negative feeling this means it is not true – it is not in alignment with the truth of GOD.

If it feels peaceful and better you have just felt the truth. We all recognise our own truth because we feel it, our soul acknowledges it and it communicates this knowing through our bodies.

Some questions we ask our bodies may be tough and the answers may take us out of our comfort zones but remember we didn't come here to be comfy we came here to expand.

"I came here to be good."

"I am broken."

"Other peoples feelings/needs are more important than mine."

"I am not loveable."

Now try:

"I came here to be..."

"I was born whole and complete."

"My feelings and needs are important."

"I am loved."

That feeling of peace in your body is the truth and you can be guided each and every step of the way if you start to trust your feelings. We need to trust our feelings, follow our hearts and not be guided by old beliefs based on fear. You are an infinite being of light but when it feels off, it's because you have temporarily forgotten this – things have got a bit foggy. The fog is simply a sign that you need to hand things back over to your inner compass. In doing so, the fog will float away and once again you will see a perspective and view that is crystal clear. It's time to trust those feelings, as feedback guiding you home – right to where you have always belonged, back to your real future.

SECTION THREE

Permission to shine

YOUR PERMISSION
TO SHINE

Are you waiting for permission?

Are you waiting for permission,
to do what lights you up?
To hear it's time to hear that you're Divine.

Are you waiting for permission to shine?

Are you waiting for permission to
write that killer song
Or stay in bed and make love all day long...

Maybe you love painting; maybe it's guitar,
or maybe it's the desire to wander afar?

Maybe it's to raise your hand and say,

'hey look at me'

Or maybe it's simply permission to BE.

Whatever permission you seek
the answer is now clear,
permission is granted once you overcome your fear.

Fear of being rejected laughed at or deplored
may keep you feeling safe but your heart will feel ignored.

But what if fear is your signal-
it's a sign that you are near,
Just take one step after another
and all will become clear.

If you give yourself permission
to have a little play
Allow your heart to guide you- listen to it say:

'Explore my darling, you may!'

The only permission that you ever need
is granted by your heart

And it shines the big green light
in the moment that you start!

44

What if nothing has actually gone wrong

What if nothing in our lives has actually gone wrong – that every single moment has been for a reason? Every moment represents a unique piece of the puzzle? No, I am not dismissing all the painful situations as necessary. I'm simply saying, what if we pause, take a breath and ask; *"What if nothing has actually gone wrong?"* Does this spark a memory, a feeling, cause an internal shift? Would it bring a smile to your face? Can you remember your Divinity and see the cosmic joke – might you hear things differently, see things differently?

That is what happened to me, I had the insight to stop and ask a better question; *"What if nothing has gone wrong but that I've just got this wrong?"* and the matrix of my own making started to shift away.

But what if getting it all wrong is the point? What if messing up is in the mix? I believe we come here voluntarily, but we go into a deep amnesia at birth and all that we know is locked safely deep inside us until the perfect moment of reactivation. It is essential we experience all we do, so we can be who we came here to be. A moment is never too soon or too late and whenever it happens it's just perfect – perfect for you and for others too. People don't need to wake up to fit in with your timeline – everyone has their own agenda, their own mission, their own moment.

So, if you are feeling frustrated with others, whom you consider are sleeping on, remember nothing has gone wrong and all you have to do is feed your own fire and follow your own heart. Look at things from this new perspective and create a magical life without needing others to validate you. Do this, and you will be the most awesome welcoming committee for those when their moment arrives.

LOVE

Love is eternal, it never goes away,
it's only a deception that makes us sometimes
think the other
way.

Love is who we are, it's everything we've got,
For us to think otherwise, is what causes the rot.

A light deep down inside us, is who we truly are
A light that's always burning, awaiting our
returning.

The more that we remember, the brighter it will glow
And then one day your fires so bright, your whole
world gets to know.

Your fire ignites another and on and on it goes
until all round loves blazing
and that, well that's amazing!

Be the spark of your bonfire heart!

Colour Your Life
Your own way

As a people pleaser this has been one of the toughest things for me to embrace. As an empath you feel everyone else's desires and this can often muddy the waters. It takes a daily practice, and even then it often isn't enough to really tune into the actual colours an empath desires in life.

Many of my flower doodles have seven or eight words, so this doodle stands out – I am struck by its clean lines and clarity. In a people-pleasing context, you get; *"The less people pleasing you do the more outstanding your life will be, your colours, your way."*

Why do we get stuck in people pleasing mode? Why do we let other people's ideas, visions and dreams, which do not align with our own, define our daily lives?

I think, somewhere along our journey we have lost faith that we are enough. We have forgotten that we are individually creative and that our choices are just as important as others. We inevitably compare and we forget how unique we are meant to be. We are so mesmerised by others whom we admire, that we try to act like them, talk like them, dress like them.

As a teenager, I remember a friend calling me out about my clothes. I had been moving between friend groups and apparently my clothes kept changing to match the group I was hanging about with. I was shocked by this revelation, but when I stepped back I couldn't deny it. Looking back, I can see this was a defining moment for me – a portal of awareness – and gradually I started to embrace what I loved to wear, regardless of the friend group. I say gradually, because it probably took until my early twenties, for me to become devoid of those strong peer groups and I started to buy my clothes based entirely on my own preferences. And, I was in my mid-thirties when a friend made the comment that I always seemed to dress in my own individual way – I was, at last, learning to colour my life, my own way.

My challenge was to do this in other areas of my life – my work life, social life, spiritual life, love life. By trying to embrace the same approach I use with my wardrobe – try new things on for size, feel and comfort – each area of my life can take on a whole new palette, and everyone is richer for it. This is the thing people-pleasers often misunderstand, yet when we do colour our life our own way it's a win, win.

It was while preparing to speak at a fundraising day about the importance of letting our inner wisdom guide us and how to ensure the insecure parts of us are not making the decisions, that I remembered the benefits of really trying things on for size, feel and comfort. Something, that could not have been further from my mind, when purchasing shoes at certain times in my life.

I'm sure we've all bought something we thought we loved when we saw it in a shop, only for it to lose its shine afterwards. Perhaps the excitement was laced with a feeling of uncertainty and doubt, but you shoved those feelings aside, and made the purchase anyway. It's only later, you realise you should have listened to the doubt.

It was late July, the summer sales were on and I was browsing the shoe department of an Edinburgh department store. I convinced myself that a pair of beautiful, sparkly shoes would make the dress I was planning to wear, to a family wedding, look glam. I tried them on, walked a few steps and convinced myself they were just right

– even if they were high, strappy, and just a tad wobbly to walk in – they would be perfect! At home I started to have real doubts – but they looked so glam I couldn't bear the thought of not wearing them. I did have another pair of shiny shoes (the far more practical wedge!) already in my closet but I stubbornly opted for the new wobbly shiny shoes. Feeling glamorous, quickly wore off after a 15-minute walk to the bus to take us to the church. And as the day and evening progressed, my poor feet did not have much fun! By choosing to wear those shoes, I was less present and did not shine in the way that I can when I am totally at home in my body. I traded what should have been a really fun, light-footed event for appearances – to strut my stuff in new shiny shoes!

This is not the only time where appearances have won. It's the mid 70s on a sunny July day. I'm visiting my Uncle's fish tackle and gift shop in the coastal holiday town of Portrush, where I bought a pair of shiny dress-up shoes. To my six- year-old self these are not dress up shoes, but real shoes and I insist on wearing them immediately. Walking along the concrete pavement, we reach the park and I'm feeling like a million dollars. I feel as if everyone around me is thinking; "oh look at the princess in those gorgeous shoes". When suddenly I hear a crack, and I am devastated, as the plastic shiny shoe reality brings me crashing down to earth and onto my bare feet. Of course I don't cry (that would be babyish) instead I just stuff down my disappointment, only for it to reappear when shopping for shoes 40 years later! Always hopeful that sparkly shoes will make her more visible – believing she needs these to shine.

I could not have been more off base when I bought the shoes for the wedding, or further away from my core desire feelings of connectedness, certainty and joy. I opened my talk for the fundraiser wearing those shoes – they were a wonderful prop – so the purchase finally paid off as I relayed the wedding story! Yet it was only in taking them off and standing in my own power, guiding people to find their core desires, that day, that the message finally got through to my younger self. You will feel more connected, you will feel more joy and certainly, be more you when you are firmly footed to this earth in your bare feet, guided by your inner wisdom. This is how you are finally able to colour your life in your own way.

46

Being you is enough, always was!

As a child my Mother would take me to see musical shows, at the senior school I would later attend, as many of my cousins took part. The standard was high, the teachers demanded a lot and expectations ran high. I can still see my older peer group singing and dancing like gods and goddesses on the stage to this day.

During my time at senior school, despite how much I loved the shows, despite how I would sing in the shower and dance when no one was looking, I never took part on stage. For a long time, it was probably one of my biggest disappointments. It all came down to the fact that I didn't think I was good enough, and I was terrified of looking stupid, of being laughed at. And because I wasn't in a show as a junior pupil, I never auditioned for future shows. I helped with ushering so I got to watch them night after night, but so much of me wanted to be on stage – yet I never experienced taking part, the thrill of the performance, the music, the dancing.

Quite simply I was not at the stage of my life of being able to be myself. It was as if I was frozen, uncertain of, who I was, so I didn't give it my all. I didn't show up as me and I let the music die inside me. All because I held my older peer group on such pedestals that being me felt totally inadequate. I thought being me was the problem. If only I could be someone else all my troubles would go away. I spent so much energy focusing on what was wrong with me that I couldn't just be.

Now as a coach, writer and speaker, I've sung on Instagram live and performed a short solo in the local gospel choir's Christmas show and I am finally understanding, with greater humility, the only thing that matters is that I show up fully. I make sure it's me that walks in the door and gives myself permission to be myself – fully, totally, completely. I show up because I am enough – it's not about whether I'm good enough.

The relief of not trying to be someone else is hugely liberating. This is what some of my peers knew all along, this is what I misunderstood. Being me is finally more than enough – for me. What about you? Do you put some people on pedestals? Are you so busy comparing yourself to them, you don't fully show up?

Being you is why you are here. There is nothing about you that has been designed wrongly, allow yourself to trust that and if you do – you will allow yourself to be. You being you, is always, and will always, be enough too.

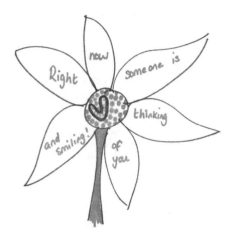

Right Now someone is thinking of you and smiling

As I write these words, certain people have popped into my mind, and a smile has spread across my face. Some of these people, I hope, know they have this affect on me but others may not. They may not even know me or have met me only a few times, but everyone has the capacity to make an impact and to bring a smile to someone's face. We are often oblivious to how we matter to others.

As humans we fall victim to believing our own thoughts and generally we would not think; *"Right now someone is thinking of you and smiling."*

But pay attention to what happens to your posture and your feelings when, you believe this thought – that right now, at this exact moment, someone is thinking of you so fondly they are smiling. You're smiling now too – your heart feels fuller you may even have straightened up a little.

Let's take it one stage further. Think of a few people, one by one, whom you like or love – don't overthink it – just allow people's faces to come to mind and see what happens to your posture, to your face. It's that smile again isn't it? I'm smiling at the thought of you smiling. What a wonderful circle of joy we have created. Just by choosing to believe this beautiful thought we have instantly raised our vibration. With that increased vibration our body is lighter, our minds are less cluttered, we feel better, about who we are – we are closer to the truth of who we are.

We are more important to people than we can ever know. We are loved and cherished, we are admired and respected, we are thought of as funny, clever, kind or compassionate. We are much more liked, than our inner critic would ever have us believe. We are never alone. We are surrounded by love from those on this earth and those not. Lean into this thought for another few moments.

This means you matter, you are loved, you being here, has an impact for good. This means you have been seen. Continue to hold this high vibrational thought close to your heart and, when you can, take a few moments to send out the healing power of that high vibrational thought to people in your life. Send a text, drop them a note or send an email. Don't underestimate the beauty of sharing this with others and don't be surprised if you hear from some of them in the next wee while because our vibrational thoughts have reach. People feel what we are thinking, so if you love someone, focus on what you love about them, focus on their smile and how it makes you feel and they will feel it from you. Take this a step further. What if right now, GOD is thinking of you and smiling – a huge adoring unconditional smile, the highest vibrational smile in the Universe. Will that give you permission to love you unconditionally too?

48

You step into your dark so that your light can shine

One night I took our dogs to the beach for a late walk, it was one of those magical still nights, we'd not had for a while, as we'd been experiencing unseasonal snow storms. Sometimes it takes a while to notice the calm, we get so used to the storm we don't expect it.

Away from the street lights darkness descended and initially I switched on my phone torchlight. But as I glanced at the sky, a smile started to spread across my face and with it, a deep sense of happiness and awe filled me, urging me to switch my light off. With every step into the dark I was rewarded with yet another star and another, and as I stood at the edge of the water all I could see above and around me was a multitude of stars dancing in the moonlight – my very own special light show.

As I stood absorbing the energy from this incredible canopy of light I started thinking about the internal journey into the darkness of our own mind that we must do, in order to switch back on all the lights from source to our soul. In my case this meant being willing to face the dark thoughts, face the shame and secrets. And, just like on the beach, the moment you take the first step in, you are instantly rewarded by a brighter internal light, a light which surpasses any artificial lights you think are there to keep you safe.

The first time a friend suggested I would make a good life coach I almost choked on my food. In my mind, I had far too many skeletons and shadows in my closet and I wasn't about to jump inside and sort them out. Of course, I didn't tell her that, I just laughed it off. But, of course, it was exactly these personal experiences which have, not only given me the joy of my own personal night time illuminations, but have helped me shine a light for others on their own courageous journeys.

We all think that our secrets and our shames are something only we have, that we are not strong enough to break free of them. My journey to becoming a coach wasn't possible without stepping into my dark, yet it was not something I thought I would ever have the courage or ability to do. In the end the fear of the life to come, if I did not step into my dark, was greater than the fear of stepping into it.

I simply had no idea how beautiful it is when you finally step into the darkness. I had no idea that in this place your light shines brightest, but thankfully my inner wisdom did. Shame and all it stifles, reminds me of this story, the author is anonymous but the tale has been retold often, as the oldest truths are.

As my friend was passing the elephants, he suddenly stopped, confused by the fact that these huge creatures were being held by only a small rope tied to their front leg. No chains, no cages. It was obvious that the elephants could, at anytime, break away from the ropes they were tied to, but for some reason, they did not. My friend saw a trainer nearby and asked why these beautiful, magnificent animals just stood there and made no attempt to get away.

"Well," he said, "when they are very young and much smaller we use the same size of rope to tie them and, at that age, it's enough to hold them. As they grow up, they are conditioned to believe they cannot break away. They believe the rope can still hold them, so they never try to break free." My friend was amazed. These animals could at any time break free from their bonds but because they believed they couldn't, they were stuck right where they were.

Our shames and secrets are like that rope and stake. Initially they are enough to stop us from moving onwards and then we think we can never escape them. We doubt our ability to break free of them and we stay amidst the artificial lights, oblivious to the fact that the real light show lies in the darkness just beyond us. Unaware of the fact, that we are stronger than we know.

I know this to be true. My relationship with my husband is now more honest and because of this I never forget how strong either of us are. I no longer keep any secrets from him, secrets which would act like the rope around an elephant's ankle. The liberation and healing effects of living in my truth, although once terrifying, proved to be life changing. I know GOD guided me to reveal all parts of myself to my husband, she guided me to trust that our world would be brighter if I broke away from the shackles of my mind. I am so so grateful I finally listened to her. She whispered to me, through the book 'The Shack' by Wm Paul Young.

The Shack represents all of our shame and shows us how we need to break out of it and reclaim the beautiful life right under our noses. I saw that without the author owning and healing his shame and breaking out of it, without him experiencing God in a new beautiful way and creating a beautiful story about it, I might still be a prisoner in my own story. The secrets stopping you from being fully present and owning that you are a loveable being, are just like rope and like rope, you can and will break free from them.

49

We heal by peeling back the layers one at a time

I have had my fair share of massages – but never with a healing intention. During my stay at Casa Fuzetta in Portugal, this changed, as the massage I experienced there felt different. The Therapist began on my legs and quickly moved to my feet. As she worked on my tummy, I realised I was not feeling at all awkward or self-conscious, in the way I might have before. I totally surrendered to her touch and my Caesarean scar and post-babies belly seemed to lap it up. I thought of American motivational author and speaker Brandon Bays who in her book 'The Journey' describes how a powerful massage played a massive part in healing a tumour in her stomach. And I wondered, if through this massage, there was the potential to release another emotional layer I might have.

Sitting, sipping tea, post-massage I noticed a beautiful glass bottle with these words engraved on it; 'The best is yet to come'. I smiled and every cell in my body seemed to vibrate. I began to wonder – what exactly was to come? The best was yet to come.

Later that day, I prepared to write my daily blog post in which I wanted to share a link to Brandon Bays. The way she works with people is very similar to the way I work with my one-to-one clients and because of my experience in the Priory I resonate strongly with her methods. What I didn't expect, as I began to research Brandon, was I was about to go on another healing journey of my own. I had a blog post to write, for heavens sake, and I was due to meet the group I was with in less than two hours!

But then I remembered our healing is actually the real work we need to do and from that place all limits are off. So, for the next half hour, or so, I lay on the bed with my eyes closed and literally journeyed with Brandon Bays in the way my clients do with me. By allowing my feelings to guide me and letting them be what they needed to be, I allowed myself to drop into my past and surround my inner child with light and love, just as I had experienced in the Priory. Without a doubt, another layer of healing took place. I could feel it in my body and it was evident as I rejoined my group later that day. Another part of me had been revealed and healed, meaning another part of me had come home. A part that now felt safe to be herself all the more.

Are you ready to peel of another layer and receive the healing?

We are in this healing journey together. Healing one layer at a time and we have the ability to do this again and again. All we have to do is follow our feelings by allowing our Divinity to guide us. You can try this exercise, but remember you can seek out an energy coach if you think you need a bit more help.

Take yourself off to a private place where you won't be disturbed. Lying on your bed is perfect or sitting on a comfortable chair.

Close your eyes and bring all your attention to your breath, and then into your body. Imagine your body is being scanned from the tips of your toes to the top of your head by a warm light and track it inch-by-inch through your body – keeping your breath even.

Now think about recent events and allow the memory of something, which has triggered unpleasant emotions (upset you, angered you) to come to mind.

Allow yourself, to feel the unpleasant feeling, but this time, allow it to flow, don't shut it down, and keep breathing through it. Now ask yourself what is underneath this feeling and allow another emotion to be experienced. Ask yourself what does this remind you of, and allow an early memory to come to mind. Keep breathing through it, and ask this part of you – what are you feeling and allow the feelings to be felt.

Keep asking this young part of you how they are feeling and what is underneath the feeling. You can also ask this part of you what he or she needs to feel better. Imagine giving comfort as your adult self.

Allowing this part of you, space to let go will peel a layer of your psychological mask and enable you be more fully you. Keep breathing through the feelings one-by-one until you feel peaceful, which you will, as long as you don't shut the feelings down.

50

Don't be limited by your thoughts

For many of us the fear of rejection still ranks pretty highly and most of us will relate to this limiting belief; *"If I ask for what I want they might say no and if they say no – I'm not sure how I'll react so it feels too scary to even contemplate."*

One day as I was walking my dogs on the beach, I spotted a couple of men dismantling the metal handrails on the stone steps, to the beach. They had special cutters and the job was completed very quickly. I remembered, I needed one of the handlebars cut off the now ornamental bike, which is attached to the staircase leading up to The Barefoot Sanctuary. Now I didn't have one of these fancy saws but in that moment I spotted a man who did. The rhetoric in my head went a bit like this; *"Oh look how quickly he's doing that – I could ask him to help me. It's perfect timing it would only take him a few minutes. Oh! He might think I'm being cheeky, he might be angry I asked. You can't ask him that, they have enough to do; they have their hands full. Blah blah blah…"*

American author and motivational speaker, Jack Canfield, in his book, 'How to Get from Where You Are to Where You Want to Be' says "The biggest difference between the people who get want they want and those that don't – is action." He explains that our thoughts and fears, which come to the fore, at the same time, stop many of us from getting what we want. In his workshops Jack sometimes stands in front of the room holding up a $100 bill. He states he is wiling to give it away, and asks if anyone would like to have it. Usually lots of people raise their hands – and do nothing else. He keeps waving the dollar bill until someone finally jumps up and takes the money from him. His teaching point is – the only thing that separated the person who got the $100 from those, that didn't, was action.

The only reason I hadn't asked the welders to help me was because my thoughts were stopping me. In Jack's story people did not want to appear greedy, they thought they might be judged or perhaps someone else needed the money more than they did. Or perhaps Jack might not hand the money over and then they would be embarrassed. I, too, thought I would be embarrassed if the welders said no, or I might even embarrass them by asking. And that's not nice – I was letting fear of rejection over this tiny thing stop me from making a simple request.

Because of what I was thinking, I decided not to ask the welders for help, but then I remembered Jack's vital message; *"How you do anything is how you do everything"*. Now I knew what was stopping me and why, I took action. I turned around and spoke to the man in charge and he was more than happy to help. He said he would; *"catch it"* that week, working around his main contracts.

When you are honest about your 'why', all parts of you show up. Even though I knew I could be rejected, I needed to get over that fear to do what I came here to do – to shine and help others shine brightly in the process.

In the end the welder didn't 'catch it'! But it motivated me to take action, on my own, rather than making it a big deal. I spent £20 on a saw and it took me less than 60 seconds to cut the handle bar off. More importantly this experience taught me that, I need to overcome many of the random thoughts, which are stopping me from asking for what I want. The more I do this, the more my 'how I do anything is how I do everything' will shift and evolve with me. The things that you put off doing, take up more energy than actually doing them.

So often the Universe puts exactly what we need right in front of us – all we have to do is take action. If we hold ourselves back in one situation, it's likely we'll hold ourselves back in another and it's time to break this pattern. Since that day, I am much better at speaking up and asking. And the more I do it, the more natural it becomes. This is one of the biggest factors in giving ourselves permission to shine – and when we do, we give other people permission to shine too.

What's stopping you from asking for something you want or need? If you're curious about this you'll discover your own patterns and you can do something about it. Once you become aware of the reasons for not acting, you can begin to overcome them. And with this, others will overcome their own obstacles alongside you.

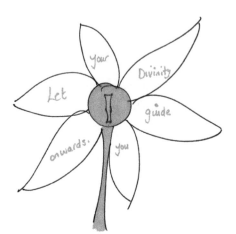

51

Let your divinity guide you

One of the biggest human challenges, we all face, is getting out of our own way and allowing the Divine presence, which resides in us, to lead. Simply saying to yourself and others; *"Get out of your own way"* doesn't necessarily help, perhaps because we take the whole thing too, darn, seriously. What if actually getting out of our way is simpler than we think? Perhaps, simply expressing how you feel is the route in – whether that's laughing, crying, screaming, dancing, writing, singing or any other creative experience. When you just let it out, you are in unison with the Divine truth that lives inside you.

When it's repressed, judged and buried, it manifests in an uglier form – where we, literally, reveal our worst fears. Things go awry, and not realising GOD is inside us waiting to come out, we can feel abandoned and lost. Yet, we have never or could ever be abandoned – there is a thread (a golden thread) so powerful, it is eternally connected for us to weave from.

God loves humour so maybe the next time you literally, laugh out loud consider this – what if that's the Divine's belly laugh?

God loves Sex so maybe the next time you feel so passionate and really let yourself go, consider this – what if that's the Divine's pleasure too?

God loves food, so maybe the next time you honour your body with delicious food, consider this – what if that's the Divine licking her lips?

God loves writing so maybe the next time you write something profound, consider this – what if that's the Divine holding the pen, or clicking away on the laptop?

God loves honouring the body's needs so the next time you yawn; consider this – what if that's the Divine requesting a nap?

God loves music, so next time you let yourself go and dance like no one is watching, consider this – what if that's the Divine rocking it on the dance floor?

What if, whenever you simply allow yourself to do what feels better or really good in the situation you are in, that is the Divine totally coming through you?

If you really want to be free to be, then perhaps it's time to totally surrender your life choices to only those in alignment with your Divine being – by doing only what feels good. The Divine guides us by what feels good, what feels right, what feels natural and truthful.

I believe the Divine gives us a clue as to where our golden thread is. In my case – my golden thread of consciousness – where the Divine has always had full control, is my love life. My love of the opposite sex caused me so much heartache as a young woman, but I always bounced back for more, and I always felt totally safe. Remember my English boy from the college ball? One minute I was all loved up and the next, my whole body, said no! When the 'no' feeling happened, I could not push against it – to do so would make me feel ill. Furthermore I have never been in danger sexually (which seems unusual when I chat with other women) and despite having had plenty of opportunity, before I was married and one occasion after, I have only ever had sex with my husband.

Looking back, I can see the Divine played a part in this – it's as if she shut down situations, which could have gone very differently. It's as if I had no choice with whom I fell in and out of love with, as a young woman. And it explains, to me, why I have only slept with my husband. It was really nothing to do with me – my eternal self was totally in charge.

I was chatting with a friend about the golden thread idea and she was trying to figure out her own golden thread. Suddenly she knew – resulting in both of us laughing out loud. Her discernment with food matched my discernment with the opposite sex. In that moment, she realised that she has never been in charge of what she chooses to eat – food needs to feel so good for her or it's a total no. As if some one else was in charge, food, which is a no, literally makes her feel sick. It was not quite the same with men for her, and for me, not quite the same with food! We will, no doubt, monitor our progress with amusement as we navigate onwards.

Ironically, it was six years after the Priory that this epiphany occurred and it took as long for me, to really trust, that the Divine communicates mostly through my body. I am now able to ignore my inner critic's nagging doubts about my marriage because if I wasn't meant to be with my partner, there is no way I could be, because she is in charge!

I left you a clue.

I left you a clue, undamaged intact

It's the thread that burns brightly

just remember to weave from that.

What is this thread, I hear you ask?

Ponder this question and then you'll know..

psst...Where did most of your cobwebs grow?

here is another clue from me to you..

*It's where you have been the most courageous,
wise and fully alive.*

*look inside and you'll know- it's your
springboard to thrive.*

*and then this journey will feel like a dance,
heck like a jive!*

Like the spider who spins, as she remembers it all

the web of your life will glisten, and shine

and the glory of you will be just Divine.

Just tap into me

search out those cobwebs,

I promise you'll see.

52

You learn to trust by trusting

I am frequently asked; *"But how do I learn to trust?"* My answer is always the same; *"You learn to trust by trusting."* Otherwise, our very inner guidance is left unused – no wonder the feeling of being lost at sea sets in when we fail to take action again and again.

We learn in this order. First, we take a leap of faith from the moment of our birth as a vulnerable baby. Then we get the chance to take 'baby steps'. From that place of trust, babies become experimental. On a physical level, as babies start to move they are willing to fail over and over – even when it hurts a little to fall, the desire to walk is so ingrained they never stop trying, no matter what.

We have to choose to trust. I can pinpoint two incidents – one with a childhood friend and one in my early sales career where my trust led to devastating betrayals. Remember, neural pathways form in pairs continuously. Due to my painful experiences, I simply didn't trust my own judgement, and when we don't, it is hard to trust others too. We isolate ourselves in the process – as the white noise becomes louder, our inner guidance is drowned out, and this is one of the most disempowering states to be in. When we trust we experience the total opposite. In the moment of trusting we experience deep inner peace, and an inner transformation of those neural pathways, and we have learnt to trust once again. And, for me, the desire to experience trust outweighed the pain caused by not trusting.

Exercise:

Close your eyes.

Take a deep breath and allow your self to travel back to a time when you trusted, yet it was sad and painful. Pay attention to how it feels in your body. Shake that off.

Now travel to a memory where you trusted but it felt really happy and light. See how that feels in your body.

There is generally a massive difference. The latter, being really positive light and warm in a certain part of your body, and the former, feeling tight and heavy in another part.

The reason I now trust my internal judgement is that both the memories of sad and happy involved trust. In my go-to memories I trusted with totally different results. Our bodies have an amazing ability to record our responses and, chances are, you will have had devastating and wonderful experiences based on trust too. Use these to navigate your way forward, trusting yourself as you go.

Remember it's okay to take baby steps into the parts of your life where things are not quite as cut and dry. Lean into the golden thread feeling, on the little things, and expand from there. Now and again a leap of faith will be required, but remember, if we follow our inner guidance by harnessing those memories and take action, we can trust that wings will appear and we will fly!

53

Don't overlook the beauty of your ordinary

By following my own yellow brick road, I have become friends with a fellow coach, Leah Cox. We have had some gorgeous moments together – our conversations are always fun and she has such a beautiful ordinary lightness about her. I think it is her ability to be present with the ordinary that is truly beautiful. One day, just as she was about to leave to head back to Lancaster, we were chatting about our lives and the beauty within the ordinary. As we chatted I looked up, and started to laugh, at a pile of ordinary contents on a tray in the living room. And yet, in that moment, it looked like a piece of art.

The contents of that tray summed up my life, so completely, in that moment. My husband's love of surfing and his sisters love of him in the gift of a surfing book. The horns my husband had bought in a second hand furniture shop, two years previously, still waiting to be put on the wall. The hyacinths, which I adore, were birthday gifts – one from my daughter, the other from a dear friend. There was a tube of hand cream, my son's headphones that were apparently 'broken' but well used, pine cones, postcards and a jar of pencils. Bits and bobs – all with an energy of the beautiful, extraordinary, ordinary life we lead.

We looked at each other and smiled at the beauty of this tray of life, which was set – or one might say dumped – on the surfing book to make room on the table, for us, at last night's supper. As we did we breathed in the blessing of being two ordinary women who five years previously had no knowledge of each other. Both creating a new extraordinary, ordinary; just hanging out together. The joy we were both experiencing of simply going with the flow of our creative lives felt very present. As we talked, Leah shared her new perspective on life – not to expend energy worrying about the small stuff in the way she used to. She knows things will work through and she embraces that life is happening in beautifully ordinary ways.

As I looked round the room – the plants in particular, despite their wilting, suddenly looked even more beautiful mixed in with these ordinary everyday objects. Ordinary life really is a unique piece of art. As I write, six months have passed, I glance up and take in the exact same view; the hyacinths are re-emerging and will no doubt be flowering by the new year. Once more, my extraordinary, ordinary life feels all the more beautiful. *"You can't stop the waves but you can learn to surf."* This is exactly what Leah realised she can do.

Take a look at your life and pause for a moment as you gaze at something in your home. Something so completely ordinary to you, take a step back from it and increase your perspective. You might see the beauty and love that is there, right at the heart of it. And, if your life is feeling like an oddly filled tray right now – never fear because, just like this tray, you are actually surfing, and from that point you can be sure you will enjoy it all the more.

54

The mission is not to impress but to express!

This is, perhaps an important reminder, which may enable us to be the most, free. Why? Simply, we must get out of our own way and express who we are. I only realised this about 30 minutes into my first visit to the art therapy room at the Priory. In fact, it was two weeks into my stay, before I realised the art therapy room even existed and, ironically, the art therapist was off for the entirety of my stay. It took a while to persuade staff to let me go there unaccompanied but as I was pretty persistent they eventually agreed.

I cringe at admitting I thought I would create a beautiful seascape, with my newly awakened Divine awareness, and immediately impress the other patient in the room. I'd previously taken art classes and along with my new inner joy I felt sure I'd impress – how wrong I was! Thirty minutes later, as I looked at my seascape, I thought; "*this is totally crap*". Feeling utterly dejected I ripped it up.

As that lovely young woman headed back to her room with her own creation, I took the opportunity to regroup and took a few deep breaths. These words came to me; "*The aim is to express, Bernie, not impress*". I thought about how I was feeling and I thought about what I wanted to express. I thought about the people I had met in the Priory who were soon to be leaving, and of my friends and family who had been sending messages to me. And, I realised I wanted to express my love and gratitude to them. I realised I was actually here to make thank you cards. I was here to express my love and thanks. The only thing that came to mind was the flower doodle I'd been drawing since I was a little girl. That flower doodle has been the Divine's way of trying to get through to me for years.

I grabbed charcoal and watercolours – a favourite of mine from my art classes – some watercolour paper and cardboard and spent the next hour or so painting poppy after poppy. In this factory-production process I was able to allow each layer time to dry before I worked on it again – impatience is a disaster with watercolours! This way I moved onto the next, then retouched and generally had a ball by playing and expressing. I chopped and I glued, and when I left – I left with 12 expressions of who I was, stacked in my arms.

I can still remember walking back to my room and the joy I experienced as I went on to express, in words, the messages to those first recipients, and the affect giving those cards had on them.

That doodle flower would be drawn, again and again, over the next three years. Then, one day, I looked at it and realised I had created the symbol of my company –Barefoot Ambition. By getting out of my own way and focusing on expressing, that first flower evolved with me. It was by expressing myself that I discovered myself.

Over the years my art has continued in fits and spurts. I often forget the valuable lesson of expressing not impressing, and each and every time I do, I produce utter rubbish. It's only when I remember it is about expression that the art flows, the words flow, she flows.

What about you? What part of you is whispering to be expressed, just for the joy and benefit of revealing that part of you? Revealing the Divinity, which lies within you, which has always been part of you. Focus on the emotions you are feeling and let them out, in whichever form feels right for you. Be it dance, yoga, music, sport, art or business. In anything you are creating, express yourself fully and by letting go of the need to impress you might just express the real truth of who you are. This is a mission, which is totally possible.

55

Don't waste energy on self-doubt

Creative energy is something we all have in equal measures. Sure, it manifests in different ways and looks different person-to-person but, essentially, we are all connected to Source so we all have access to the exact same amount of energy. My realisation in the art room that self-doubt blocks our expression got me thinking; *"Why do some people get described as creative whilst others don't?"*

There are layers to this and other factors at play – how we absorb energy and how we use our own energy. Every minute of every day we have the choice to be connected to the Source of all energy, and yet, how we use it will have different results. So why does self-doubt use up this precious resource?

I am sure most of us use a smart phone, and although you start the day with a 100% battery – there are some days when, before you know it, you are out of juice. And have you thought; *"But I've hardly done anything with it yet?"* Then you discover, yes, you are connected to the WiFi but you left your mobile data on!

Self-doubt is like data – round and round it goes in your mind thinking it's being helpful but at the same time draining you of your creative juice. When, all the time you could be using that direct dial connection. Just as with your mobile phone data, you need to switch self-doubt off, each and every day, when it is simply not helpful – that way you stay connected to the unlimited creative Source that lies deep within you.

Any time you find yourself pausing and not taking action – it's because your self-doubt is whirring around in a loop using up vital reserves.

If you look at people you admire in the world, it's sometimes easy to think they have more talent, more creative ability than others less accomplished. But this is not necessarily the case. They are just more disciplined at switching off self-doubt and they are not waiting for permission from others to express who they are. They feel the fear but take action anyway – they will have taken baby steps before they took leaps. Trust yourself to take baby steps too.

In every day, in every way, you have the ability and the right to self-express – doubt is something, which comes with the package. Once you accept this, you don't have to let it drain you of your creative power.

56

Connect to your body stand in your power

Bluetooth is a wonderful thing – I used it daily for a while to send photos of my flower doodles from my phone to my computer so I could add them to my blog posts. Of course, in the process of doing this, I am opening up my computer and phone to other Bluetooth devices in the immediate vicinity. One day as I was attempting to do this in a local café someone else's phone came up – in that moment they were, unknowingly, open to receiving stuff from me.

What has this got to do with standing in your power? We are energetic beings, we feel things in our energy field very easily and we, unknowingly, operate in Bluetooth mode. Meaning, we can, inadvertently, receive stuff from people in our vicinity – leaving us feeling depleted and exhausted.

As an empath this is one of my biggest challenges, and the single most important thing I need to remember is – to connect to my body so I can stand fully in my power in any situation. I want to remain open to feel all the beauty around me, but I need to make sure I am fully connected to my internal source first and foremost, so others cannot come into my energy field uninvited. Remember the energy vampires? Without that invitation you are totally safe.

A few days later, I spoke to a young woman who describes herself as an introvert. She admits to becoming easily overwhelmed and drained when around a lot of people. Immediately I realised that on these occasions it is, as if her Bluetooth is on, and not just one, but tons of people, who also have their internal Bluetooth on were coming into her energy field. Meaning she feels really drained being in a room with others, without even talking to them. This had happened, to her, in an exam situation. She was in a much bigger exam room, than expected, and in the moment of overwhelm she disconnected with her body. Of course, she was concentrating on a test paper which will have used up some of her energy, but she was also feeling all the emotions of those in the room – she was wide open and it was no wonder she felt so drained afterwards.

The key to solving this is preparation. We need to be aware if we are leaving our energy fields wide open, just as we need to be aware if we have left the Bluetooth on. This does not mean you put up a wall around yourself – rather you automatically create a beautiful energy bubble around you when you fully connect to your body. Before you head out to public places, which may leave you open to being unnecessarily drained, it's worth spending a few moments connecting to your feet and then mentally surrounding yourself with an expansive bubble of light. Feel it around you, like a protective magnetic shield, but one, which stops people taking from you without permission. As you feel the warmth of this bubble around you, in your minds eye, see yourself in a busy room feeling totally energised and powerful. In this bubble you are connected to Source and, the good news is, others around you will feel the benefit but they won't drain you. It's as if you have activated an energy bubble that simply feels good to be around but cannot be pilfered from. Even if you forget to do this, and find yourself in a situation where you suddenly feel overwhelmed and experience a feeling of powerlessness, you can pause – reconnect with your breath, reconnect with your body and allow the bubble to reemerge and the overwhelm will float by.

This is a very important part of self-care. You feel things deeply and you have to take responsibility of retaining your own energy levels. Others will keep their Bluetooth on around you and there is nothing wrong with this. You just need to make sure you are taking control of your own – so that you are always standing fully in your power.

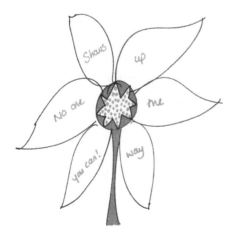

No one shows up the way you can

From the moment of birth the seeds of our uniqueness, the seed of our great essence is already firmly planted deep inside our soul. Because of this, together with your unique human experiences, no one can show up the way you can. These experiences are essential so you can show up – fully, wholly, completely, imperfectly. If you have ever seen someone truly be themselves, embracing all of who they are, you can genuinely feel it – it's easy to watch them, it's easy to be around them. Our inner guidance feeds back to us that this is genuine, this is real. When someone tries to copy someone else or imitate their way, therefore hiding their true self, we instantly feel it, through the same feedback – it just feels off.

We all have our unique parts and the important thing to realise is, in this life, no understudy will do. No one can play us authentically, so if we don't play the part we came here to play, it simply can't happen. Don't underestimate the importance of being you – the way only you smile, the way only you laugh, the way only you frown, the way you light up when you do the things you love – when you connect with people in your unique way. And this world really does need you to show up – wholly, fully, imperfectly in the way only you can.

You do this by letting go of labels and by peeling off the layers of imitation, by letting go of who you think you should be. You need to let go of thoughts such as; '*I should*', '*they will think I'm*' and '*if only I could be like*'. It really is up to you to be you!

Do you really believe that a mistake has been made in your creation? Do you really think that you have not been given the innate gifts and the exact human experiences necessary for your adventure? I'm not talking about an easy life. I'm talking about your human adventure. You need to reclaim your power by letting go of comparisons and letting go of doubt. We can show up as who we truly are – all we have to do is to stop trying to be who we are not, and let our divine essence shine through.

58

Don't be afraid of who you are

For centuries, we have all been misled into thinking we should be afraid of our dark side. From a very early age, in many religions, we are told we are born of sin and we need to be forgiven and saved – to ensure entry into heaven. And, only then will we be fully at peace. But even if we are all children of God – we have to be the 'right religion', be part of the approved tribe, and it's not safe to reveal our true identity in certain situations.

That's a pretty dark thought and it certainly doesn't feel empowering. It's never felt right for me and it's no wonder that many of us who experienced this programming feel confused. We criticise ourselves, and are constantly vigilant to what, we falsely believe, that we are a soul hardwired for sin and therefore feel unworthy.

Instead of this programming, allow yourself to become still, just for a few moments, and without any judgement feel the peace that really does live inside of you. Give yourself permission to lean into this. Take a few deep breaths, allow yourself to stay very still, then gently look at your hands and feel the presence there. Now put your attention to your feet and feel the presence there also. You can experience peace right here, right now, in your present moment. This is the presence of who you really are. This is you, experiencing heaven on earth.

What if we are simply here to experience who we really are and add to this beautiful expanding Universe which we are co-creating?

We are of GOD and we are GOD and we add to this beautiful Universe by allowing ourselves to feel everything, rather than shutting down our emotions and to experience what these feelings create over and over again without judgement.

Unfortunately, many of us keep our feelings hidden at certain points in our life and this often happens in our formative years. It is these events, which can keep us stuck and hold us back from truly being ourselves. And, could be the reason why we hate parts of ourselves.

I was 13-years-old and visiting my best friend in Cookstown, Northern Ireland, during the summer holidays. We had known each other from the age of four and even though she had moved away, when I was seven-years-old, we remained close and every summer I spent time with her and her parents. We were now at high school and both our social groups and the politics of Northern Ireland were increasingly harder to ignore. Also harder to ignore, was that I always compared myself to her and felt dull alongside her. My friend looked completely different to me, and her religion, in Northern Irish terms, was the polar opposite – I was Catholic and she was Protestant. Because of the segregated educational system, in Northern Ireland, so were all her school friends and many of them, if not all of them, did not mix with Catholics.

That summer, together with one of her friends, we set off to a roller disco in a neighbouring town. My friend, an only child, had a wardrobe to die for and seemed to be emerging into the teenage years effortlessly. In comparison my clothes choice felt inadequate – hand-me-downs from my older sister. My outfit, feeling okay at first, was actually totally impractical for roller-skating and I felt too skinny and awkward in my dress and winkle picker shoe combo.

In hindsight, I can see that introducing me, by name, might have caused problems. And, it must have dawned on my friend, that evening. In Northern Ireland, the name Bernadette is obviously a Catholic name. And, in Northern Ireland, one of the ways we tell a person's religion is by their name, a habit that would stay with me into my early thirties.

Of course, as young children this had never been a factor in our friendship and I didn't see it coming. That evening, my two companions quickly rushed off without me to chat to a large group and I found myself alone, wishing the floor would swallow me up. Previously I had loved my trips to stay with my friend, now I was wishing I could do a 'Dorothy' and click my heels together to get back home. Of course I couldn't, so I tried to look unflustered and to hide my growing discomfort by pretending to nonchalantly watch the skaters, whilst sitting on a ledge – as my feet were now really uncomfortable.

I would later blame the shoes for my feelings but I was soon to feel totally ungrounded. One of boys came over to talk to me – he seemed nice enough but I certainly didn't fancy him – and I was flabbergasted by his opening line; *"Hi Helen how do you like our roller disco?"* At first, I thought I'd misheard him, but very quickly I realised he truly believed he was calling me by the right name. I don't know why but a feeling of fear inside said *'play along'*. Without giving myself away, I managed a pretty awkward conversation but for the rest of the evening I felt numb.

I was desperate to speak to my friend to find out what was going on, but she avoided eye contact with me at every opportunity. As we left, the other girl pulled me further up the road, and told me what I hoped wasn't true. They had given me a different name, as there would have been 'trouble' if, it was discovered a Catholic was out with them.

This was my first experience of the damaging effects of the religious divide. Up until that point, religion had not been a dividing factor in my life – all through my childhood I'd had Protestant friends. I was devastated and confused. The boy who thought I was called Helen looked like any of the boys I knew at school, so what was it, that suddenly made us different? Would they really have turned on me? My friend and I never spoke about it. I think she was probably as devastated as I was, and in some ways it marked the end of our innocence and we gradually grew apart. I began to hate the sound of my own name and, in the months that followed, in an attempt to block the pain, I reinvented myself as Bernie. The part of me who was Bernadette was clearly not enough and I would do my best to forget about her too.

What I realise, today, is that all of us that night, were victims of the religious bigotry that separates us in our hearts and minds. The people of Northern Ireland, of all faiths, have a lot in common with each other, but their warmth and essence is often disguised because of the old story of religious divide. I have spent time with, and experienced warmth and love from many people on both sides of the community, which helped heal my wounds. But none more so, than the realisation that we are all truly beings of light and ideas in the mind of God, and nowhere in God's mind are any of us different. This is human invention – that's the illusion.

Being terrified of the dark side and, in my case, the supposed dark side of others as I was in my youth, is a real energy-zapper. It drains us and keeps us stuck and small. What if we have never actually been in any real and present danger? What if it's just distracting from the fear that we are actually most afraid of our light?

Our programming is so strong – that to be considered worthy or magnificent, to be so much more than we can ever imagine – terrifies us the most. So we inadvertently keep ourselves small and we stay asleep to the truth. But, the evolved part of our being has never been afraid. It is just letting us experience all that we are not, so we can experience more fully all that we are, and that is the actual experience we desire.

The self love work I do and help others do involves healing emotional wounds layer-by-layer, letting go of who we are not and embracing parts of us stuck in the past. The scared, youthful loving non-judgemental parts and the stubborn parts of our teenage selves will surely be fun companions as we adventure on.

What hidden parts of you, do you need to own and heal? Because being who you are and expressing yourself fully is the most precious gift you can give yourself and from there, all good things will come.

With a new half century waiting for me, not using my full name is not embracing and loving the small child that adored the name. She really liked it and it was who she was, and over the last few years it has begun to sound so different to my ears and feel more like me.

We will not fail in remembering who we are; it's as inevitable, as the fact that the sun will shine. But if, in this incarnation, we want to make a difference in the here and now, it's up to us to step out of the shadow of our small story – sooner rather than later – and reignite the flame inside. We are the ones who can shine our light so brightly that it will eventually feel safe to step out of the shadows. This is our quest and I trust it's not impossible.

59

I want to be
well known

These are the words, I heard the late David Bowie say, as a replay of an old interview re-aired on the radio, when news of his departure from this world took momentum. In this brief insight in to his success, Bowie was telling the interviewer that sometime, early in his creative career, he had been asked; *"Why do you want to sing?"*

Up until this point he had been performing mime, painting, writing songs and singing. What's interesting is, he didn't necessarily think he was a good singer and yet, it was this question, which seemed to give him greater clarity and focus. He realised, in that moment, and finally admitted honestly to himself, his why. Which he later recalls, with a chuckle, during this interview – the reason he wanted to sing was because he wanted to be well known!

What an honest answer and it would seem that in being honest with himself, and understanding his why, his future path became clear. What's your why right now? Give yourself permission to shine a light on that why.

In the lead up to my breakdown (breakthrough!) in 2010, I was due to be interviewed by a local paper about a new business venture I was involved in. At the briefing, a couple of weeks before the interview was to take place, I was told; *"They just want to know why you became* involved in the business, the personal story." As painful as that whole experience was, I will be forever grateful, because upon hearing those words I knew the game was up. I realised I simply didn't feel authentic with 'my why' and not being honest would destroy me. It was as if my body would have thrown up, had I lied about my why.

If the interview had gone ahead and I had answered honestly, this is what I would have said; "*Part of me is really excited about this business because I think it will make me rich. It's a wonderful idea but I can also see that I don't honestly believe I am good enough to do anything else right now. I'm too afraid to admit that something feels off inside. I'm not smart enough or brave enough to be honest about how I really feel, and deep down I don't know what to do about it. Oh my God, I'm really not well, am I?*"

Of course this didn't happen, but inside me it did. Because of that question my internal communication system went into warp speed. Our bodies don't lie to us, they won't sustain our own nonsense and, consequently, an emotional crash became inevitable. With the interview looming, it was as if the cogs of the Universe orchestrated things so perfectly to bring things to a head, that in one week I discovered more about myself than I had in my whole lifetime. It was, literally, as if I had been blind, and now I could see I realised that my thoughts about me, and the world had been my biggest problem. I stepped into my darkness and GOD switched on the light. That question took me further down the path of self-discovery and like all good roller-coaster rides, has been scary at times and painful. The truth really will set you free.

My why today?

I want to be me, and more than anything else, I want to be well. I want all parts of me to feel loved and well known. That is the gift that writing and life coaching has given to me – I meet myself in my written pages and I meet myself in my clients. The healing for all of us is priceless.

I want to know myself and deepen the love that I have for all parts of myself which might still believe they are inadequate. I want all of those parts of me to know the truth, that they are enough, and in doing so I trust my message will become well known and will benefit others too. Whether it's through my writing, and speaking, or in my day-to-day interactions with people, this burning message of love and truth, and our real divinity is what fuels me. By loving the imperfect human being that I am, I hope to inspire as many people as possible, who currently aren't loving themselves to embrace showing up in this world, as themselves just as they are. Permission to shine a light on my truths can only come from me. Owning all the flawed parts of me, although sometimes painful, and owning the parts of me that are pretty wonderful is the best present I can ever give myself and it will be for you too.

A couple of years ago when I was on holiday, in Australia with my family, I received an email from an American based coach offering me the chance to take part in a tele-summit with other life coaches. I was, of course flattered, (this was tapping into my 'well known') and their message resonated; yet I knew nothing about them or their reach. I didn't have the 'this is so exciting' feeling, but at the same time it felt interesting and necessary to see where this was going. I agreed to an initial talk with the host, but only upon my return home. I felt pretty pleased with myself and I even thought; *"Hmm my reach is obviously growing as clearly someone wants to share what I say with more people."* I can be very naive but my plan was, to just show up, and see what happened. Turns out I didn't need to show up, because at the eleventh hour I was uninvited. It turns out my 'reach' was not yet big enough!

My first thoughts were; *"Ah I knew there was a catch"* and my inner critic said; *"na na na na na!"* which I let float by. But then I saw the gift, I smiled at me, at my inner critic and the words of David Bowie echoed in my mind; *"I want to be well known."* But this time, it was with a clear certainty, that I want to be known well first. I want my message to be understood clearly and not with a minimum list criteria. I only want to be part of something where the experience of me will be valued first, so my soul will be known well because I am making being me and being well my priority. And only then, because of a real sense of purpose, will I be well known. The almost-but-not-quite invitation to the tele-summit served its purpose beautifully as I discover my soul's why. The following year, when I did actually take part in two tele-summits, they felt amazing and I, honestly, felt so well and grounded during both experiences.

For the rest of my life I plan to let my soul show up and lead me even more than before. I will work at letting the Universe guide me forward, as it already does perfectly, making the rejection experience feel like a gift.

So what's your why?

Are you at the stage where your why is full of holes? Do you know your why, but have yet to fully embrace and go with it? It does, of course, mean there is a fresh bunch of limiting conditioned beliefs ready to be blasted – but this is what this experience is all about. Go on, look inside you, what is your secret why? Give yourself permission to get curious. Say it out loud, write it down in a private place, or email it to me directly. What is the why which will give you permission to shine? I know it will feel scary but I really believe this world's desire is that you let yourself be seen for, who you really are - a bright being of love and light. As I've said many times, you simply can't get this wrong sweetheart.

60

Shine and from here all good things will come

This book is about us all – so many people relate to the thoughts and doubts that I have had. This book is about us all giving ourselves permission to shine. To not write this book, would serve absolutely no one. We all want to be known well and we all deserve to know who we truly are.

Remember, I was afraid of auditioning for parts in my school musicals. I was so afraid of being laughed at, and so convinced I wasn't good enough that I didn't give it a go. I am now fully convinced the 'gods and goddesses' performing in those musicals were also afraid – they felt fear, they just didn't let it stop them. They had enough faith that it didn't matter if someone laughed – and of course, no one did laugh. Their desire just ebbed slightly higher than their fear.

My mid-life awakening allowed me to look back at my many lost opportunities, based on fear. And through this self-awareness, I have been pushed to do many of the things I had been too afraid to do in my younger years. That's why getting to know yourself really well is key in being able to shine. Fear is still there every day but it feels as if the balance has been tipped and I'm more in control as the CEO of my life.

Small children are often afraid of new things and they rely on their parents for assurance, that they can take these brave steps forward. Now I am actively choosing to have faith in the Universe, I lean on that, in the same way I must have done with my parents and older siblings as a young child. I have simply returned to choosing faith – faith that I am safe and that I am held in a loving guiding energy. The message has always been the same, if we stumble it will be okay, and if we tune into our body we can tell the difference between real and imagined fear. But it's always a choice. We all have the chance to start over, we all have the chance to choose, to lean into the help right inside of us. And just like a little child we can choose to take baby steps towards fearful things.

More than anything, I hope that this book reawakens, or adds in some way to your understanding, that keeping yourself small serves absolutely no one. You can only heal the parts of you that are afraid, and you are never alone in trying to do so. By healing these parts you are giving yourself permission to shine in the way that only you can and in the way, deep down you know you came here to.

And no one knew this more than best selling New York author, Debbie Ford. On the fifth anniversary of her death and written during her long battle with cancer, 'Your Holiness' is a thoughtful and poignant exploration of the godliness that resides in all of us. From the moment I read her opening prayer I could feel her loving guidance and I refer to the prayers almost daily. For me, these words became more alive, in relation to my message to you, because they sum up why the Universe wants us to give ourselves permission to shine:

"There is nothing else for you to do but truly love your inner self. That's what you were given. That's your job on the planet; to deeply love, respect, admire, and nourish your precious self, the spirit that only you hold. That is the antidote, the answer, and the solution out of which all good will come." – Debbie Ford

About the author

Bernadette Petrie is a Life Coach, Speaker and Spiritual guide based in the seaside town of North Berwick on the East coast of Scotland. She is the founder of the Spiritual wellness centre The Barefoot Sanctuary which opened in April 2014 and the Creator of The Barefoot Talks which began in 2015.

Bernadette's life changed course following her own spiritual awakening in 2010. This sparked her own healing journey and her ambition to live an authentic soulful life. She has been writing her blog called Barefoot Ambition since 2013. Permission to Shine is her first book.

Along side the Operational and Creative aspects of the Barefoot Sanctuary, Bernadette offers 1-1 coaching sessions in person or by phone. She also runs regular workshops and weekly compassionate meditation classes at the Barefoot Sanctuary.

Bernadette is originally from Northern Ireland, and she moved to Nottingham England in 1987 and then to Glasgow in 1992. She has lived in North Berwick with her husband and children since 2005.

Email: bernadette@barefootambition.co.uk

http://bernadettepetrie.com

http://www.thebarefootsanctuary.co.uk

http://www.instagram.com/bernadettepetrie/

https://www.facebook.com/bernadetteamp/

https://twitter.com/bernadetteamp

Acknowledgements.

To my Husband David, thank you my love for staying on this adventure with me, and for your constant love and support.

Thank you, to my parents Ann and Luke and my parents in- law, Alison and Anthony. To all of my siblings, Maria, Thomas, Damian, Paul, Emma and Claire- and the invisible essence of Joan – we are quite a pack- I wouldn't have had it any other way. To the Mullan/ Mckenna clan and the PetHoWiToWa clan –family means so much to me, and I'm proud to be a part of yours. You are all in my heart.

To my dear earth 'Angels', that are made up of old and new friends, that know my heart and have shown me theirs. I see your 'ness' and am constantly touched by your ongoing love and support.

Thank you, to my barefoot community of blog readers and Local Life readers - your feedback and encouragement, enabled me to hone my writing skills and find my voice. Thank you, to all of my coaching clients, and the wonderful team of past and present Practitioners from the Barefoot Sanctuary – You have all helped me grow, and enable me to do what I love. A special thank you to anyone who ever asked me "how's the book coming along"? I really needed that accountability.

This extends also to my amazing peers, the support and encouragement from other coaches, healers, writers and speakers that I have connected with, over the last nine years, means so much to me. Whether in person or via the web, you each made a difference to how I show up as Bernadette today. Thank you to the Alisoun Mackenzie Mastermind Group, that I had the joy of getting to know, and growing with. This was sparked by my desire to work more closely with two amazing women, already in the group, Julie Begbie and Jennifer Main. I am so glad I followed through with that.

Timing is everything, so I want to give thanks to coaches Maja Karlsson and Tabitha Benway. Taking part in both of their online tele-summits in 2018 almost back to back, cemented the creation of the title; Permission to shine. The summits also revealed to me just how much the flower messages could resonate with a wider audience. As has being a part of the Detox Health Beauty Festival, where I, The Barefoot Sanctuary and the Barefoot Talks have been given an amazing platform to shine from- thank you Sheena Skinner!

To Kim Williams, my amazing Editor- both here and in her Local Life magazine. You really are a genius! My intuition chose you and I see why, as you have sculpted my message so beautifully – thank you, thank you, and what fun we had in the editing process! Let's do it again!

To my brother, Damian Mullan, of So it Begins Design, for all the graphics, making this book look as good as it does, and for your constant support in the branding of The Barefoot Sanctuary. Thank you D!

To Kim & Sinclair Macleod of Indie Authors World, thank you for your patient, encouragement, honesty and guidance, thereby getting this book into the world. Doing this with you feels so good!

To Jo Turner, thank you for proof reading the final edit for me- you are so good! Your support and enthusiasm, for the work I do, has been such a tonic. I am so glad, that we had such a beautiful conversation, the first time we met, which led to this happening.

I would also like to thank the staff and fellow patients, who were either working or staying at the Priory, where life re-began during my stay there in 2010. They each played an important part in my healing journey.

The following coaches have all helped me on own coaching adventure via their personal coaching, online courses or podcasts: Louise Trevatt and the Simply Changing team, Melody Fletcher, Martha Beck, Amy Aylers, Dr Lissa Rankin, Marie Forleo, & Debra Poneman. Closer to home, thank you to coaches and guides; Alisoun Mackenzie, Neil Francis, Christel Rosenkilde Christensen, Bernie Rowen-Ross, Lizzie Martin, Fiona Morris, Nicole Reid and Toni Reilly, for their unique guidance and encouragement during the long process of writing of this first book.

I appreciate greatly the spiritual inspiration I gained from Lendrick Lodge – it is a place of magic. In particular, spiritual teachers, Stephen Mulhearn, Vicky Mulhearn, and Peggy Dillon.

My own healing journey has shown me that people I thought were the problem where actually part of the solution. Quite a turnaround. It has also shown me that often the people who had the biggest effect on me, where 'supposed strangers'- 'angels' in disguise. There are so many people who have helped shape me, solid proof of the ripple effect. I am so grateful, that all of them, played their part so perfectly.

Over the last nine years, I have discovered even more guides, and mentors via their own written work and podcasts; each have helped me to believe in myself and my message. Many of their books and podcast links you can find listed in the book reference section – I encourage you to dive in as feels good to you, they all have so much wisdom to share.

Book references.

Foreword

Neale Donald Walsch: *Conversations with God volumes 1-3*

T1.

The Full Complete Text: *A Course of Miracles*

Marianne Williamson: *Return to love*

T4.

Andrea Gardner: *Change Your Words Change Your World*

T8.

Melody Fletcher: *Deliberate Receiving -Finally the Universe Makes Some Freakin Sense*

Dr Bruce Lipton: *Biology of beliefs*

T12.

Brené Brown: *Daring Greatly*

Byron Katie: *I Need Your Love - Is it true?*

Iyanla Vanzant: *Tapping The Power Within*

The Course of Miracles

T14.

Wm Paul Young: *The Shack*

Super Soul Conversations: The podcast by Oprah Winfrey (see iTunes)

T15.

Netflix: *Once upon a time*

Byron Katie: The Work www.byronkatie.com

T16.

Wm Paul Young: *The Shack*

T17.

Neale Donald Walsh: *God's Message to the World: You've Got Me All*

Wrong

T20.

Amy Aylers: *Reform Your Inner Mean Girl*

Dr Lissa Rankin: *Mind Over Medicine*

Martha Beck: *Finding Your Way In A Wild New World*

T21

Jack Canfield: *How To Get From Where You Are To Where You Want To Be*

Eckhart Tolle: *The Power Of Now*

T22.

Marianne Williamson: *From Tears To Triumph*

Robert Holden. Lovability – *Knowing How To Love And To Be Loved*

T24.

Netflix: *The Vampire Diaries*

T26.

Andrea Gardner: *Change Your Words, Change Your World*

T27.

Marianne Williamson: *A Year Of Miracles*

T31

Jennifer Main: *The Space Between*

Alisoun Mackenzie *Heartatude – The 9 Principles Of Heart-Centred Success*

C.S Lewis: *Voyage Of The Dawn Treader*

T34.

Martha Beck: *Finding Your Own North Star*

Martha Beck: *Expecting Adam.*

T35.

MGM Movies: *The Wizard Of Oz*

T37.

Melody Fletcher: *www.melodyfletcher.com*

T42.

Esther and Jerry Hicks: *The Vortex - The Teachings Of Abraham*

T48.

Wm Paul Young: *The Shack*

T49.

Brandon Bays: *The Journey*

www.brandonbay.com

T50.

Jack Canfield:*How To Get From Where You Are To Where You Want To Be*

T60.

Debbie Ford: *Your Holiness*

Other recommending reading and resources

Podcasts:

The Beautiful Writers Podcast by Linda Severstein.(itunes)

Marie Forleo: *B School www.marieforleo.com*

Other suggested books:

Eckhart Tolle: *A New Earth*

Echkart Tolle: *Stillness Speaks*

Dr Lissa Rankin: *The Daily Flame*

Neale Donald Walsh: *Happier Than God*

Gary Zukav: *Spiritual Partnership - The Journey to Authentic Power*

Anita Moorjani: *What If This Is Heaven?*

Danielle La Porte: *White Hot Truth*

O.R Melling: *People of The Great Journey*

Dr Bruce Lipton: *The Honeymoon Effect*

Kim McMillen: *When I loved Myself Enough*

Gay and Katy Hendricks: *Conscious Loving*

Neil Francis: *Changing Course*

Neil Francis: *The Entrepreneurs Book*

Michael A. Singer: *The Untethered Soul*

Louise Hay: *You Can Heal Your Life*

Mike Iamele: Enough Already

Gary Chapman: *The Five Languages of Love.*

Mastin Kipp: *Daily Love Growing Into Grace*

John Niven: *The Second Coming*

Elizabeth Gilbert: *Big Magic*

Elizabeth Gilbert: *Eat, Pray, Love*

Tabitha Jayne: *The Nature Process*

Rebecca Campbell: *Light Is The New Black.*

Glennon Doyle Melton: *Love Warrior*

D. M Green: *Jim and The Universe*

D.M Green: *Eva and The Universe.*

Seth Gardner: *Taming Amy*

Dr Lori Leyden: *The Grace Process Guidebook*

Ainslie Macleod: *Instruction Living The Life Your Soul Intended.*

Eckhart Tolle: *Milton's Secret: An Adventure of Discovery Through Then, When, and the Power of Now*

Byron Katie: *A Mind at Home with Itself: Finding Freedom in a World of Suffering*

Dr David Hamilton: *I Heart Me, The Science Of Self Love*

Toni Reilly Awake: *The Purpose Of Life And Why You Are Here*

Fay Johnstone: *Plants That Speak, Souls That Sing*

Robin Rice: Do Overs – An Irish Story

Robin Rice: *Venus For A Day*

Catherine de Courcy : *An Adventure In Grief*

Catherine de Courcy : *Montségur – A Novel*

Charles Eisenstein: *The More Beautiful World Our Hearts Know Is Possible*

Kim Macleod: *From Heartbreak To Happiness*

Mitch Albom: *Tuesdays With Morrie*

Dr Susan Jeffers: *Feel The Fear And Do It Anyway*

David Schwartz: *The Magic Of Thinking Big*

James R. Doty: *Into The Magic Shop*

Dr. Tim Cantopher: *Depressive Illness, Curse of The Strong*

Lightning Source UK Ltd.
Milton Keynes UK
UKHW020659090619

344113UK00005B/148/P